Timesaver Project Work

Janet Hardy-Gould

Teacher's reference key

Level

The number of stars on each page tells you the level of each activity.

Students with one or more years of English

Students with two or more years of English

Students with three or more years of English

SCHOLASTIC

MARY GLASGOW MAGAZINES

Contents

Introduction

Timesaver Project Work is a rich resource of lively photocopiable materials for English teachers to use with secondary school students aged 10–15. The easy-to-use worksheets save preparation time and form an ideal bank of supplementary materials to complement any course book. The activities range from engaging reading and writing tasks to fun communication activities and board games. Each project has simple step-by-step stages that guide students to the final outcome. At the back of the book there is also a full **Answer Key**.

Why use projects?

Clear goals for students

The projects in this book provide students with a motivating opportunity to practise their English in a meaningful context. Each project has a clear goal such as designing a cool outfit, organising a fun class quiz or developing a new theme park. The results can give learners a real sense of achievement and enable them to understand how English is used in a wide range of realistic contexts.

Consolidation and skills practice

Project work allows students to consolidate the language that they have learnt and encourages them to acquire new vocabulary and expressions. In addition, it gives learners integrated skills practice. Throughout *Project Work* students have extensive practice of the key skills of reading, writing, listening and speaking.

Cross-curricular links

Using projects with classes also provides excellent opportunities for cross-curricular work. For example, in *Project Work* you will find projects with strong links to the subjects of drama, art and design, history, mathematics and the natural sciences.

Motivating topics

Project Work is ideal for supplementing course books and providing students with extra language practice around given themes such as fashion, pop music or celebrities. The topics have been carefully chosen to appeal to teenage learners and are all presented in a lively and up-to-date manner.

Something different

The projects in this book are a wonderful way of bringing something new and different into the classroom. They can be integrated into a weekly curriculum or used on special occasions such as the end of term. Many of the language areas in the book reflect the main grammar and vocabulary components of a typical curriculum. Project work is a good way of bringing variety to a course *and* improving key language and skills.

Teamwork

Finally, a large number of the activities within the book encourage students to work in groups or pairs in order to create and develop something new and unique. The projects suggested can help provide a strong team feeling within a class and engender a good working atmosphere. Bringing out the essential creativity in learners can lead to a focused class with a positive sense of purpose.

How to use this book

The worksheets can be photocopied for use in the classroom, and many are also suitable for self-study and homework.

- The book is divided into seventeen individual projects at three different levels: elementary, pre-intermediate and intermediate. The projects for students at an elementary or pre-intermediate level consist of three pages of worksheets; the projects for students at an intermediate level consist of five pages of worksheets.

- At the beginning of each project there are **Teacher's notes**. These provide a clear guide to the following:
  - the level
  - the language focus
  - an indication of the time required to complete a project. Projects can be done during consecutive lessons or continued over a longer period of time with some of the work carried out at home.
  - the topic
  - the skills that are being practised
  - the key vocabulary that students will encounter and learn
  - the materials that the teacher needs to bring to class
  - what the teacher needs to do before the lesson in terms of photocopying etc.
  - a simple step-by-step guide to the stages in the classroom

- The first project in the book, **Project 1: Let's get started** provides a lively introduction to useful language for doing projects in the classroom. It includes a special cut-out section of expressions to put up on the classroom wall.

- At the back of the book, there is a **Glossary of useful expressions** (page 94), which students can use when doing projects.

- At the end of some projects, there are optional activities to provide follow-up work on the same topic.

Abbreviations used in the Teacher's notes

Abbreviation	Meaning	Example
adj	adjective	long
adv	adverb	loudly
n	noun	actor
phr	phrase	a long time
phr v	phrasal verb	wash up
v	verb	discover

How to do projects

Choosing a project

There are a number of different approaches to choosing a project for your class. You can select one which fits in with a particular vocabulary or topic area that students are studying. The **Teacher's notes** at the beginning show the key topic for each project. For example, if students are focusing on the subject of food, you can incorporate all or parts of **Project 8: My own restaurant** into your weekly timetable.

Alternatively, you may wish to choose a project to go with a certain area of grammar. For example, **Project 6: Famous people from the past** is an excellent way of consolidating students' understanding and use of past tenses. The contents table also has information regarding the main grammatical areas covered in each project.

Finally, a project can be selected to give students specific skills practice. For example, **Project 3: Come to a party!** would provide useful practice in reading for specific information for a class of elementary students.

There are, of course, other important factors to take into account when choosing a project, such as the level and interests of your students. If you find two or three suitable projects for your class, you could consult the students themselves on which one they would prefer to do.

When to do project work

Projects can either be carried out as part of an ongoing course or used on special occasions such as the end of term. One popular way of using a project is to exploit it to consolidate grammar or vocabulary covered in a previous lesson. Students can have the opportunity to practise and refine recently learnt language.

Alternatively, you may wish to use project work as a series of revision lessons at the end of a key stage in the course. You can use the project to revise a wide range of previously learnt language while at the same time feeding in some new expressions and vocabulary.

Another way of approaching project work is to set aside one or two hours every week, for example, Friday morning, to do an ongoing project such as **Project 17: A class website**. This will enable students to carry out individual research as part of their homework.

Remember that you don't always have to do a whole project from this book. The materials are specifically designed to be adapted and modified for shorter mini-projects if necessary.

Setting goals for students

Before setting up a project with your class, it is essential to explain the final outcome. This will help the students to understand what they are doing and why. For example, if you do **Project 9: Where I live**, explain to students that at the end of the project they will write and design a small leaflet about their town or area.

Starting a project

It is important to present a new project in an enthusiastic way and engage the class actively in a discussion about the key topic area. This can be done in a wide variety of ways using pictures, maps or personalised questions about the subject matter. For example, at the beginning of **Project 10: Aliens from outer space!** it would be worth spending time exploring the opinions and ideas of the class about this topic. The more students are engaged in and committed to a project, the more likely it is that the project will be a success.

Seating arrangements

The layout of the classroom can be instrumental in creating a positive working atmosphere for project work. For example, if you wish the class to work in small groups, rearrange the desks, with a table in the middle, so that students are sitting facing each other. This will facilitate face-to-face interaction and encourage cooperation. It is often a good idea to nominate one student as the group 'secretary' to write down notes and assist in focusing the others on the task in hand.

The teacher's role

Your role as teacher will change and develop according to the stage of the project. In the early stages, you will need to spend time explaining important points to the whole class and clarifying any new language. As the project moves on to the stages where learners are required to create something, your role will change to that of monitor, resource and facilitator. While students are busy working, circulate around the classroom helping them with vocabulary and useful phrases. Try to encourage learners to think of their own ideas rather than imposing your opinions. The students may not always produce what you had in mind but the key thing is that they will have been engaged in the learning process and have produced something of their own!

Giving students time to plan and think

Planning time is very important in project work. Don't be afraid to set aside a quiet five minutes when students can think and note down ideas on a piece of paper. This stage can help provide a fruitful exchange of opinions when the class is then put into pairs or groups to work on a particular task.

Encouraging the use of English

During project work it may not be realistic to expect your class to use the medium of English all the time. When students become very involved in the active stages of a project there is bound to be some use of their own language. However, it is important to encourage the use of English and this can be done in a variety of ways:

- Before doing your first project with students at an elementary or pre-intermediate level, do the activities in **Project 1: Let's get started**. These are designed to help students learn classroom expressions which are useful for doing project work. You will find in this section a page of expressions designed to be put up on the classroom wall. You can refer students back to these expressions during further project work sessions.
- At the back of the book, there is a glossary of expressions for use in particular situations, such as playing board games or suggesting ideas in groups (**Glossary of useful expressions**, page 94). Go through the relevant phrases with your class before doing an activity.
- Before you start a project, discuss with students the importance of using English. When monitoring activities, remind students to try to speak English most of the time.
- Nominate an 'English monitor' in each group or pair to encourage the use of English during a particular task.

Using dictionaries

It is a good idea to encourage the appropriate use of dictionaries during key stages of project work. This will promote independence and enable learners to make quick progress with their task. Students can use bilingual or monolingual dictionaries depending on their level.

Recording vocabulary

Project work provides many valuable opportunities for students to learn new vocabulary and expressions. Encourage your class to start and maintain vocabulary notebooks or lists where they write down useful new words that come up. You can support this by writing vocabulary on a special section of the board.

Researching projects

Research is an important aspect of many of the activities in this book. Depending on the resources available in your school, projects can be researched using a variety of ways. Students can use the following:

- reference books and encyclopedias from the school or public library
- current newspapers and magazines
- the internet
- electronic reference materials such as encyclopedias and dictionaries on CD Rom

When using the internet ensure that students use a suitable search engine such as *Alta Vista*, *Google* or *Ask Jeeves* in order to start looking for information. One of the best search engines for younger learners is *Ask Jeeves for Kids*: ajkids.com. With these search engines students can type in key words or ask simple questions. Encourage them to make their searches fairly specific so that they do not spend too long looking for information.

Correcting project work

It is often a good idea to do projects in separate stages. This can give learners the opportunity to prepare and write a rough draft of their work and give it to you for correction. Using the symbols in the table on page 9 **(Correction symbols for written work)**, you can make notes on students' work and encourage them to make the corrections themselves. This can be done in class or as homework. Work carried out in stages with time for redrafting will result in a more satisfying final outcome.

Giving feedback

Always give your class positive feedback at the end of a project. It is a good idea to have a final stage where students can see the work that others have produced. Many of the projects in this book culminate in a classroom display or final activity which can give the students a real sense of pride and achievement.

Correction symbols for written work

Symbol	Meaning	Example
^	Add a word.	My mother is ^ doctor.
\	This word is not necessary.	We went ~~at~~ home early.
P	Punctuation	Where do you live **P**
Sp	Spelling	She is my best **Sp** freind.
WW	Wrong word	My mother is a good **WW** cooker.
WO	Word order	He has a **WO** black small cat.
T	Tense	I've **T** been to the cinema yesterday.
Gr	Grammar	Is this **Gr** yours pen?
#	Number	Marco and Gabriella **#** is Italian.

Project 1: Let's get started

Teacher's notes

Note: This project is to prepare students for doing the project work activities in this book.

Level Elementary/Pre-intermediate

Language Asking for objects, classroom language

Time 90 minutes

Topic Classroom objects

Skills development • Listening • Speaking

Key vocabulary dictionary (n), elastic band (n), felt-tip pen (n), glue (n), (pair of) scissors (n, pl), paper (n), paper clip (n), pen (n), pencil (n), pencil sharpener (n), repeat (v), right (adj), rubber (n), ruler (n), sellotape (n), spell (v), stapler (n), wrong (adj)

Materials Classroom objects, e.g. pens, glue, sellotape etc.

Before the lesson Photocopy:
- 1 page 11 (**Classroom objects**) per student.
- 1 page 12 per pair of students. Cut as shown and enlarge if possible.
- 1 page 13 (**Classroom language**). Cut as shown.

The lesson

1 Ask students to take out some everyday objects from their bags such as pens, rubbers, felt-tip pens etc. In pairs, students discuss what the objects are in English. Bring in extra objects in case some students don't have any.

2 Give each student a photocopy of page 11 (**Classroom objects**). Students match words and pictures on their own. After a few minutes encourage students to work with a partner. Go through answers as a class. Check pronunciation. Demonstrate how to ask for the objects in class using: *Have you got …, please? Could I borrow …, please? Could you pass me …, please?* Check the use of *a, an, some* and *the* in this context.

3 In pairs, students do an information gap activity using the same vocabulary and expressions. Students need to find four classroom objects that neither of them has in the pictures on page 12. Give Student A in each pair a photocopy of the top half of page 12. Student B receives the bottom half. Students are not allowed to look at their partner's photocopy.

4 To start with, each student looks at their own picture individually. They need to identify the nine objects that they <u>don't</u> have on their 'desk' and circle the relevant pictures on the side. For example, Student A will circle a dictionary, rubber etc.

5 Students then sit back to back and ask their partner for the nine objects they don't have using the phrases on their photocopy. For example, Student A asks: *Have you got a dictionary?* If Student B has the object, they can say: *Yes, of course. Here you are.* In this case, Student A puts a tick next to the picture of the dictionary on the side. If Student B doesn't have the object, they say: *No, sorry. (I haven't got one.)*

6 The aim of the activity is for students to find the four objects that neither of them have. These are: a rubber, a pencil sharpener, a paper clip and some sellotape. When everybody has finished, students can ask the teacher for these missing objects.

7 Now move on to the **Classroom language** section. Ensure you have cut up the sentences on page 13. Elicit each sentence one by one using mime, gesture and key words. Drill for pronunciation. Then stick the sentences up on the board and draw a small picture/write key words to reflect the meaning of each sentence next to each one. For example:
- *Sorry, I don't understand.* Draw a face with a question mark.
- *Can you repeat that, please?* Draw a rewind symbol. ◀◀
- *What's 'café' in English?* Draw a face and a thought bubble with the British flag and the word 'café'.
- *Have you got a pen, please?* Draw a face and a thought bubble with a pen.
- *What does 'computer' mean?* Draw an unsure face and a thought bubble with the word 'computer'.
- *How do you spell 'friend'?* Write F-R-I-E-N-D.
- *Can you help me, please?* Draw a picture of student with their hand up.
- *Is this right/wrong?* Draw a tick/cross.

8 Gradually take the sentences away one by one, leaving just the pictures or key words. See if the students can remember the original sentences. At the end, put the sentences back up and ask students to copy them into their notebooks.

9 At the beginning of the next lesson, see how many of the sentences the students can remember without looking at their notes. Put the signs up permanently near the board. Give students points during their lessons when they use any of this classroom language.

10 When doing the project work activities in this book, encourage students to use the language learned in this project so that they speak in English as much as possible.

Classroom objects

What are these things called in English? Match the words to the pictures.

- a pair of scissors
- a paper clip
- some glue
- some paper
- a dictionary
- a pencil
- some sellotape
- some felt-tip pens
- a rubber
- a pencil sharpener
- a stapler
- a ruler
- a pen
- an elastic band

1 *a pencil*

2  ....

3  ....

4  ....

5  ....

6  ....

7  ....

8  ....

9  ....

10  ....

11  ....

12  ....

13 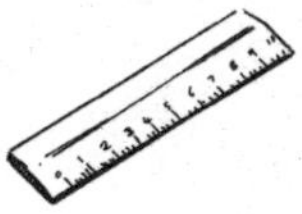 ....

14 ....

Student A

Look at the things on your desk. Then look at the things you need. Ask your partner for the things you do not have.

You need:

What are the four missing things?

....

Have you got ...?

Could I borrow ...?

Could you pass me ...?

Student B

Look at the things on your desk. Then look at the things you need. Ask your partner for the things you do not have.

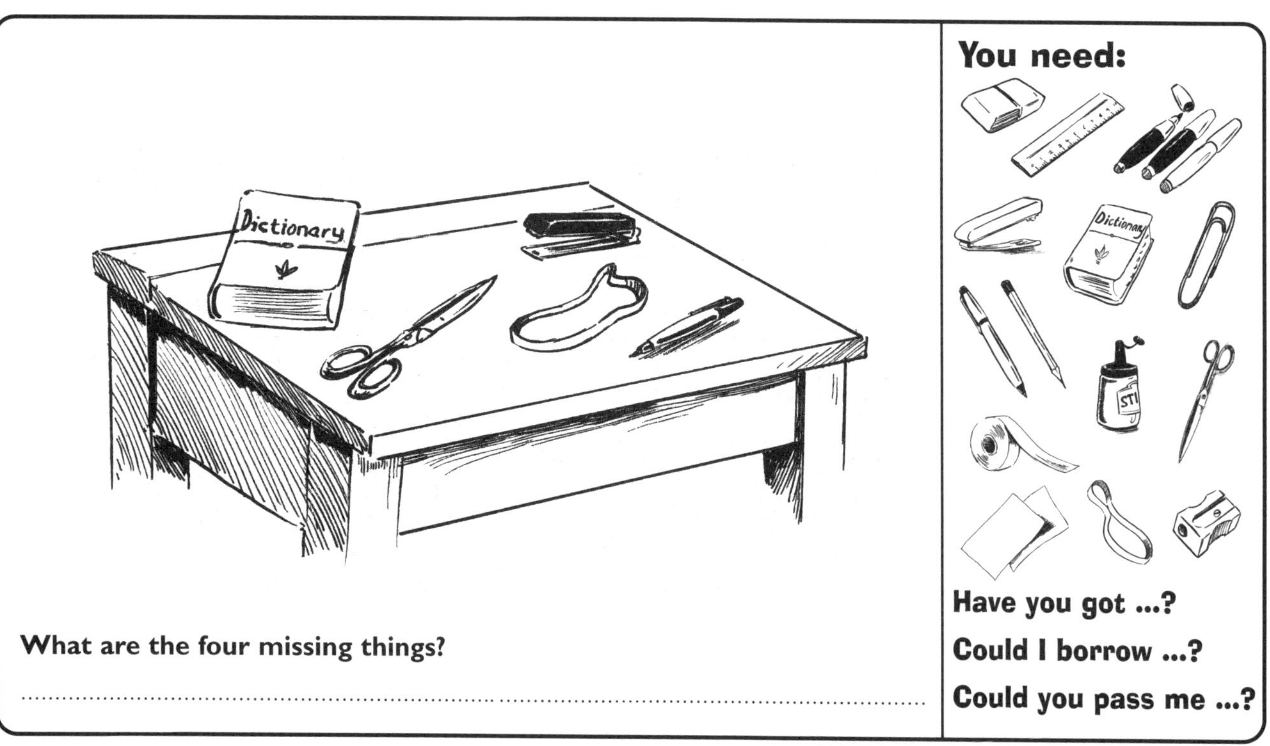

You need:

What are the four missing things?

....

Have you got ...?

Could I borrow ...?

Could you pass me ...?

Classroom language

Sorry, I don't understand.

Can you repeat that, please?

What's 'café' in English?

Have you got a pen, please?

What does 'computer' mean?

How do you spell 'friend'?

Can you help me, please?

Is this right/wrong?

Project 2: All about us

Teacher's notes

Level Elementary

Language Present simple, *have got*, likes and dislikes

Time 120 minutes

Topic Penfriends, personal information

Skills development
• Reading • Writing • Speaking

Key vocabulary age (n), cat (n), dislikes (n, pl), dog (n), favourite (adj), hate (v), likes (n, pl), love (v), lucky (adj), penfriend (n), pet (n)

Materials
- Coloured pens
- Passport photo of each student (optional)

Before the lesson Photocopy:
- 1 page 15 (**Letterbox**) per pair of students.
- 3 sets of **Questions** on page 16. Cut as shown.
- 1 **Interview with Sylvie** on page 16 per pair of students.
- 1 page 17 (**Factfile**) per student.

The lesson

1 Explain the word *penfriend* to students. Ask if anybody has a penfriend. Elicit personal information you would put in a penfriend section of a magazine.

2 Give each pair of students a photocopy of page 15 (**Letterbox**). Ask example questions about the penfriends: *How old is Antonio?* (Twelve). *Where does Dimitris live?* (Korinthos, Greece.)

3 Now use the **Questions** on page 16 to do a reading race. Put the questions (three sets) at the front of the class. One student from each pair runs to the front, takes a question and then returns to their partner. They find the answer and write it down. The student then returns the question and takes another until they have finished. The winning pair finishes first and has the most correct answers.

4 Ask students to cover their photocopy of page 15 (**Letterbox**). What can they remember about Sylvie from France? Elicit information. Now give each pair of students a photocopy of the **Interview with Sylvie** on page 16. Students make questions by putting the words in the correct order. Then they match the questions to the answers. Conduct feedback carefully. Ask students for full answers to the questions, e.g. *My name's Sylvie Deschamps. I'm fourteen years old.*

5 Students now make posters about another person in the class. Give each student a photocopy of page 17 (**Factfile**). Go through the categories on the factfile. As a demonstration, individuals could ask you questions and you write your answers on the board (your name, likes/dislikes etc.). Give students a few minutes to make rough notes about their possible answers to the categories. Monitor the class, help with vocabulary, spelling etc. Encourage them to refer back to page 15 (**Letterbox**) for ideas. In pairs, students interview each other. Students answer the questions with full sentences: *My name's George. I'm twelve years old.* However, their partner just writes the basic information on the poster:
Name: George
Age: 12
Students complete the factfile for their partner in pencil.

6 Students do a final corrected version in pen and attach a photograph or draw a picture of their partner. They can design and colour a border to go around the edge of the poster to reflect their partner's likes/dislikes, e.g. small footballs, tennis racquets etc. Put the posters up in the classroom for everybody to read.

Optional activity

Students choose a penfriend from the magazine page and reply with a short letter of introduction.

Letterbox

Find a penfriend.

Hello everybody!

My name's Janina. I'm 12 years old and I live in Lublin in Poland. I've got two sisters called Kassia and Alina and a dog called Olly. I've got blond hair and blue eyes. At weekends I love going to parties with my friends. I don't like getting up in the mornings and I hate tidying my room!

I'd like to have penfriends all over the world. Please write to me!

Janina Starzewski
Box 558

Hi!

I'm Dimitris, I'm 13 years old and I'm from Korinthos in Greece. I've got brown eyes, dark hair and I'm tall. My favourite sports are basketball, football and swimming. I also like playing computer games and watching MTV. I haven't got any brothers or sisters but my best friends are George and Nikos. I play football with them every day.

I'd like to have penfriends from Italy, France or Spain. Bye!

Dimitris Kaloudis
Box 376

Hello!

My name is Antonio and I'm from Verona in the north of Italy. I'm 12 years old and I've got a brother called Adriano and a sister called Isabella. I'm interested in music, travel and pets. I go to school near my home. This is my first year studying English. I'm also learning French and German.

Write to me soon. I'd like to receive letters from all over the world.

Best wishes,
Antonio Lazaro
Box 608

Hi!

I'm Sylvie from Toulouse in France. I'm fourteen years old and I've got a twelve-year-old sister called Camille.
I love going to the cinema and playing tennis with my friends. I'm interested in cooking and my favourite food is pizza. I don't like walking to school or going to the dentist! I like animals and I've got a cat called Mimi. I've got green eyes and dark brown hair. My favourite colour is yellow and my lucky number is three. What about you?

I'd like to have penfriends from a lot of different countries.

Love,
Sylvie Deschamps
Box 238

Send your letter with the box number to: Mary Glasgow Magazines, Commonwealth House, 1–19 New Oxford Street, London, WC1A 1NU, England.

Questions

1 How old is Sylvie?

2 Where does Antonio live?

3 What are Dimitris's favourite sports?

4 What colour is Janina's hair?

5 What is the name of Sylvie's sister?

6 Who is studying three languages?

7 Where does Dimitris want a penfriend?

8 What does Janina hate doing?

9 Who likes tennis?

10 Who has got a brother and a sister?

Interview with Sylvie

Questions

1 name / your / is / what
What is your name.............? (i)

2 old / how / you / are
.............? ( )

3 colour / what / eyes / got / you / have
.............? ( )

4 live / do / where / you
.............? ( )

5 brothers / have / got / sisters / any / and / you
.............? ( )

6 do / you / what / doing / like
.............? ( )

7 like / what / don't / you / doing
.............? ( )

8 favourite / food / is / what / your
.............? ( )

9 colour / favourite / your / is / what
.............? ( )

10 lucky / what / number / is / your
.............? ( )

Answers

a Fourteen.

b Green.

c Pizza.

d Going to the cinema, playing tennis and cooking.

e Three.

f Walking to school and going to the dentist.

g Toulouse, France.

h Yellow.

i Sylvie Deschamps.

j Yes. A sister called Camille.

Factfile

Name ______________________

Age ______________________

Town ______________________

Hair ______________________

Eyes ______________________

Brothers and sisters ______________________

Likes ______________________

____

Dislikes ______________________

____

Favourite colour ______________________

Lucky number ______________________

Favourite food ______________________

Favourite pop star ______________________

Project 3: Come to a party!

Teacher's notes

Level Elementary

Language Imperatives, dates, times, prepositions of time

Time 120 minutes

Topic Parties

Skills development
• Reading • Writing • Speaking

Key vocabulary activity (n), barbecue (n), equipment (n), fancy dress (n) football kit (n), ghost (n), guest (n), Halloween (n), invitation (n), host (n), party (n), pillow (n), pyjamas (n, pl), sleeping bag (n), swimming stuff (phr), witch (n)

Before the lesson Photocopy:
- 1 page 19 (**Party invitations**). (Cut into separate invitations. Enlarge if possible.)
- 1 set of questions (**Questions**) on page 20 per pair of students.
- 1 **Party invitation** on page 20 per student.
- 1 page 21 (**Party planner**) per group of students.

The lesson

1 Ask students what type of parties they know or have been to. Aim to elicit the following words and phrases *fancy dress party, sleepover party, Halloween party* and *barbecue* as well as other types of party. Establish party vocabulary including *guest, invitation* and *host* and the expression *RSVP* (from the French 'répondez s'il vous plâıt':'please reply').

2 Put the **Party invitations** on page 19 up around the classroom. Give each pair of students a photocopy of the questions (**Questions**) on page 20. Go through the questions and check any problems. Present the following words: *football kit, swimming stuff, sleeping bag, towel, pillow.* Then ask students to walk around the room, read the party invitations and find the answers to the questions. Alternatively, give each pair of students a photocopy of page 19 (**Party invitations**) and ask them to read them sitting at their desks.

3 Check the answers to the questions. Then quickly copy invitations 1 and 3 on the board and go through the format of an invitation. Revise all the possible beginnings of an invitation: *Come to a party! You are invited to a party! We're having a party! It's party time!* Go through the sections *Date, Time* and *Place* and highlight the use of *to, at, on* and *from.* Point out the use of the imperative: *Come* … . *Don't forget* … .

4 Tell students they are going to plan their own party. As a class go through the **Party planner** categories on page 21 and brainstorm ideas for each section. For example, under *Food*, elicit different things to eat at a party. Note: *Activities* could be games or dancing and *Equipment* could be things like a CD player or a barbecue.

5 Put students into groups of four and give each group a photocopy of page 21 (**Party planner**). Students plan their own party and a 'secretary' completes the worksheet.

6 Give each student a photocopy of the blank invitation on page 20 (**Party invitation**). Ask them to design and write an invitation to the party they have planned in their group. They could invite another student or someone from a different class.

7 A representative from each group tells the rest of the class about their party and the invitations are passed round. At the end, students could decide which party they would like to go to. Finally, make the invitations into a wall display.

Party invitations

❶

Come to a Halloween party!

To Chris
Please come to my spooky party!

Date Saturday 31st October

Time 7 o'clock

Place 25 Castle Street, Oxford

Don't forget to wear fancy dress!
Come as a witch, a ghost or even Dracula!

From Alex **RSVP** Tel 583622

❷

You are invited to a party!

Dear Chris

You're invited to a sleepover party at my house.
Please bring a pillow and sleeping bag.
Don't forget your pyjamas!

Date *Friday 16th October*
Time *8 o'clock*
Place *19 Grange Road, Oxford*
From *Billy*

Let me know if you can come. Call me on 582996.

❸

We're having a barbecue!

To Chris
Come to a barbecue party at Hill Street Outdoor Swimming Pool.

On Saturday 29th August

At 2 o'clock

Please bring your swimming stuff and some food for the barbecue.

From Katie and Jo

RSVP Katie on 587340 or Jo on 586451

❹

It's Party Time!

To *Chris*
It's my birthday! Please come to a football party.

At *North Road Sports Centre*

On *Thursday 17th September*

From *6.00 to 8.00*

Don't forget your football kit and a towel!

From *Max*

RSVP ***584430***

Questions

Which party ...

1 is for a birthday? *Number 4*
2 starts at 8 o'clock? ....
3 is in the afternoon? ....
4 is fancy dress? ....
5 finishes at 8 o'clock? ....
6 is at a sports centre? ....
7 is all night? ....
8 do you need a swimsuit for? ....

Party invitation

To ____________________

Date ____________________

Time ____________________

Place ____________________

____

From ____________________

RSVP ____________________

Party planner

Party hosts ....

Type of party ....

Place ....

Time ....

Date ....

Number of guests ....

Type of dress ....

Food ....

Drink ....

Music ....

Activities ....

Equipment ....

Other notes ....

....

Project 4: Design a new outfit

Teacher's notes

Level Elementary

Language Clothes, adjectives to describe clothes, colours

Time 80–100 minutes

Topic Clothes and fashion

Skills development
• Reading • Writing • Speaking

Key vocabulary belt (n), checked (adj), coat (n), collection (n), designer (n), football kit (n), earring (n), jacket (n), jeans (n, pl), long (adj), necklace (n), outfit (n), shirt (n), shoe (n), short (adj), skirt (n), slogan (n), striped (adj), sweatshirt (n), swimsuit (n), T-shirt (n), tracksuit (n), trainer (n), trousers (n, pl)

Materials
- Fashion pages from a magazine
- Coloured pens

Before the lesson Photocopy:
- 1 page 23 per group of 4 students. Cut into cards as shown.
- 1 page 24 (**Young designers of the year** and the set of clothes at the bottom of the page) per pair of students. Cut as shown.
- 1 page 25 per student. Cut the clothes out.

The lesson

1 Bring fashion pages from teenage magazines into class. Show students the pictures. Elicit clothes they like to wear and clothes vocabulary in English.

2 Put students into groups of four (three to eight students in a group is also all right). Give each group a set of cards (picture cards and word cards) from page 23. Ask students to work together and match the words to the pictures. This could be done as a race. Go through the answers as a class. Check the pronunciation of words and the meaning of the following adjectives: *checked, striped, long* and *short.*

3 Now tell students to put the picture cards in one pile and shuffle them and the word cards in another pile and shuffle them. They then put the set of word cards in a row on the desk and the picture cards in another row and try to memorise their position. After that, they turn both sets of cards face down. In groups, students play 'pairs'. One student begins by turning over a picture card and then a word card. If they match, the student can take the 'pair' and have another go. If they don't match, the student must put the cards back in the same place and the next person has a go. The idea is to remember where the matching words and pictures are on the desk. The winner has the most 'pairs.'

4 Now put the class into pairs. Give each pair a photocopy of **Young designers of the year** on page 24. Pre-teach the following words: *collection, designer, football kit, outfit, slogan.* Ask students to read **Young designers of the year** and say what type of clothes each designer creates, e.g. modern, romantic etc.

5 Give each pair of students a photocopy of the pictures of the clothes on page 24. Students guess which designer created the different clothes. Feedback as class. Students justify their ideas.

6 Tell the class they have won a competition to create an outfit with one of the designers. Each student chooses a designer from page 24 (**Young designers of the year**) they would like to work with.

7 In pairs or alone, students design their own outfit. They can use a similar style to their designer or develop their own style. Give each student or pair of students a photocopy of page 25. Students can choose a template from this page, e.g. the football kit, and draw round it onto plain paper. Then they add the rest of the outfit such as trainers and socks. Students write a detailed description of the outfit with the price and where it can be bought, e.g. *This is the new London United football kit. The top is red and white. The shorts are black with big red stripes. You can buy it in all Olympia football shops. It costs 60 euros.*

8 Display the students' outfits on the wall. Ask the class which one they would like to buy.

Optional activity

In groups, students organise their own fun fashion parade with clothes brought from home. One person from the group can commentate while the others walk up and down.

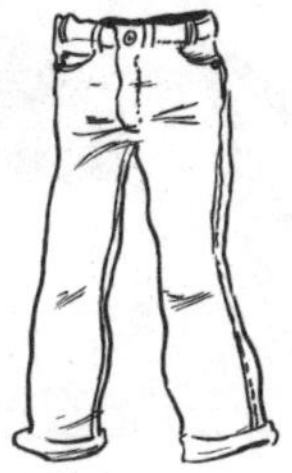

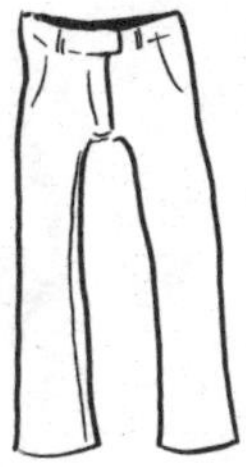

belt	checked shirt	coat	earrings
jacket	jeans	long skirt	necklace
shoes	short skirt	striped shirt	sweatshirt
tracksuit	trainers	trousers	T-shirt

young designers of the year

Yvette Laurent

Age: 28

Nationality: French

Clothes: Yvette designs romantic clothes for the modern woman. Her new collection has beautiful tops, skirts, hats and dresses.

Colours: Pink, yellow and white.

Best outfit this year: Romantic top and long skirt with large yellow flowers.

Marco Rossi

Age: 25

Nationality: Italian

Clothes: Marco designs sports clothes for men and women. His new collection includes swimsuits, shorts, T-shirts and sweatshirts.

Colours: Dark blue, light green, big black and white stripes.

Best outfit this year: The new football kit for a famous Italian team.

Ella McCarthy

Age: 24

Nationality: British

Clothes: Ella makes clothes for young men and women to wear to the coolest clubs in town. Her new collection also has earrings and necklaces.

Colours: Red, black, silver and gold.

Best outfit this year: Short dress for clubbing.

Alvin Shine

Age: 22

Nationality: American

Clothes: Alvin makes modern clothes for young men and women. This year's collection has T-shirts, jeans, hats, cool trainers and sweatshirts with big slogans on the front and back.

Colours: Bright yellow, orange, light brown and black.

Best outfit this year: White jeans and a big sweatshirt with 'New York' slogan on the front.

1 

2 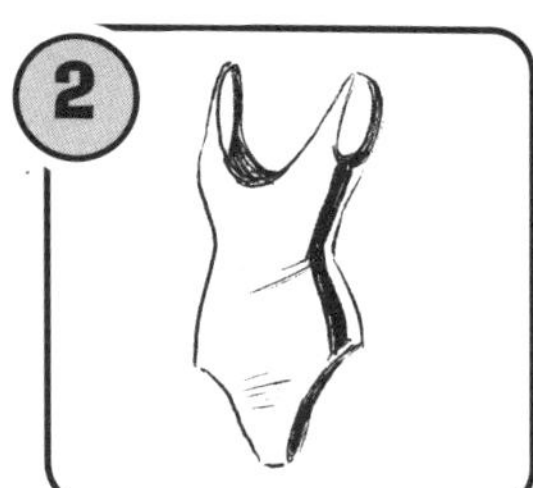

3 

4 

5 

6 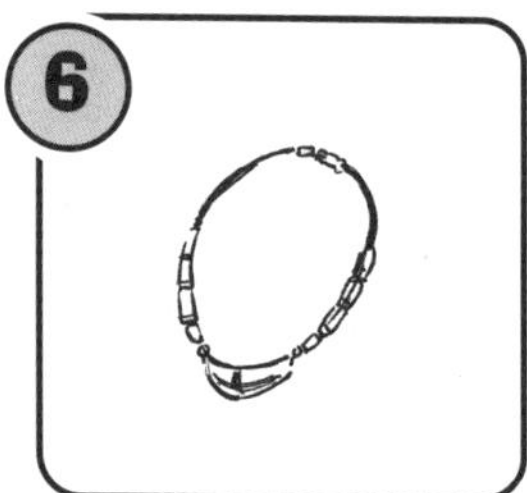

7 

8 

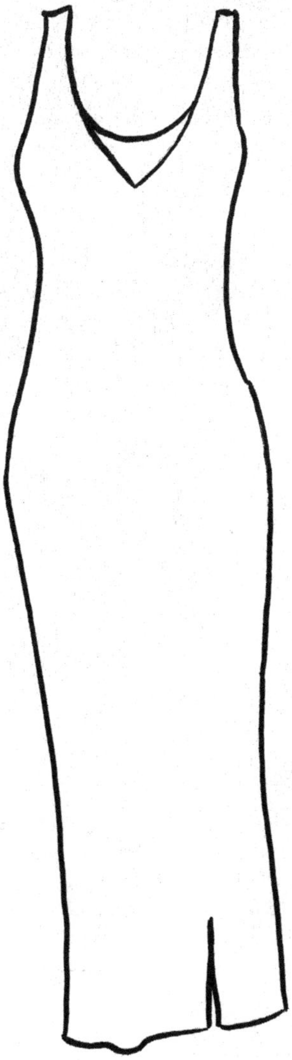

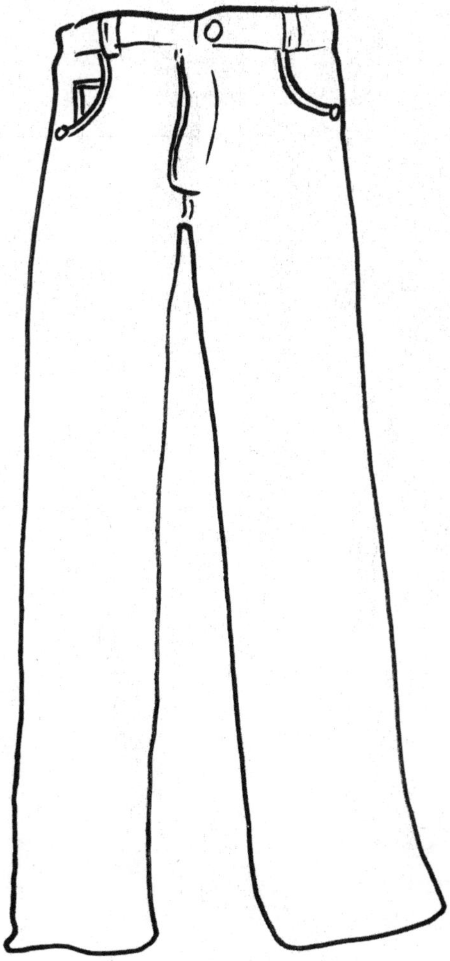

Project 5: A class quiz

Teacher's notes

Level Elementary

Language Present simple and past simple questions, question words, superlatives

Time 120–150 minutes

Topic General knowledge

Skills development
• Reading • Writing • Listening • Speaking

Key vocabulary actor (n), baseball (n), building (n), bridge (n), capital (n), emperor (n), food (n), general knowledge (n), genius (n), geography (n), giraffe (n), history (n), invent (v), library (n), nature (n), Planet Earth (n), pasta (n), player (n), potato (n), rice (n), river (n), science (n), song (n), team (n)

Materials
- An atlas of the world
- An encyclopedia (optional)

Before the lesson Photocopy:
- 1 page 27 (**Are you a general knowledge genius?**) per pair of students.
- 1 **And now ... the answers!** on page 28 per pair of students.
- 1 **Five-minute quiz!** on page 28 per pair of students.
- 1 page 29 (**Write your own quiz!**) per group of 4–5 students.

The lesson

1 Establish the meaning of *general knowledge quiz* and explain to students they are going to do one. Ask which subjects they know a lot about, e.g. football, pop music, the cinema etc. Put students in pairs and give each pair a photocopy of page 27 (**Are you a general knowledge genius?**). Check the meaning of the word *genius*. Quickly go through the questions and explain any unknown words. Tell students not to call out answers.

2 The class does the quiz in pairs.

3 Give each pair of students a photocopy of **And now ... the answers!** on page 28. Students can correct their own answers or those of another pair and calculate the score. Go through the answers as a class. Students find out which category they are in.

4 Put the class in different pairs. Give each pair a photocopy of the **Five-minute quiz!** on page 28. Get them to cover the answers. Go through the categories and questions. Explain any unknown words. Students then uncover the answers and see if they can match the questions to the answers in five minutes.

5 As a class go through the answers. Highlight the form of the questions and the use of different question words, e.g. *who, what, where, how many*.

6 Put students into teams of four or five and ask them to choose a name for their team. Give each team a photocopy of page 29 (**Write your own quiz!**). Each team thinks of two questions per category and writes them on the worksheet. (Students at a lower level can do one per category.). Refer the class back to the **Five-minute quiz!** for examples of question types. Students can look at an atlas or encyclopedia to check their questions. Monitor and help students.

7 Now do the quiz. Team A begins and asks their first question. The members of the other teams discuss the answer and put up their hands when they are ready. Decide which group was first; they have the first chance to answer. If their answer is correct, they get two points; if it is wrong, they lose a point. A second team can now try but they only have one point for a correct answer. Then it is the turn of Team B to ask a question and so on. Put the scores on the board. Remember your decision is final!

Optional activity

Students write a general knowledge quiz in English for the school magazine or notice board. There could be a small prize for the winners.

Are you a general knowledge genius?

Answer the quiz below and find out!

1 Where was the singer Kylie Minogue born?

a the United States
b New Zealand
c Australia
d Canada

2 Where is the longest river in the world?

a South America
b Africa
c North America
d China

3 How many players are there in a basketball team?

a five
b seven
c nine
d twelve

4 What is the food *paella* made from?

a potatoes
b rice
c pasta
d chocolate

5 What is the capital of Australia?

a Sydney
b Brisbane
c Melbourne
d Canberra

6 When did Alexander Graham Bell invent the telephone?

a 1875
b 1895
c 1925
d 1955

7 The Williams sisters are famous tennis players. What are their names?

a Venus and Selena
b Venus and Serena
c Vanessa and Selena
d Vivian and Helena

8 Who was the first president of the United States?

a Abraham Lincoln
b Thomas Jefferson
c George Washington
d John F Kennedy

9 How fast can a tiger run?

a 26 km an hour
b 36 km an hour
c 46 km an hour
d 56 km an hour

10 *Feijoada* is a type of food. Where does it come from?

a Brazil
b France
c Germany
d India

11 How far is the Earth from the Sun?

a 14 million km
b 40 million km
c 114 million km
d 149 million km

12 Which of these *isn't* in New York City?

a the Empire State Building
b the Statue of Liberty
c Golden Gate Bridge
d Central Park

And now ... the answers!

1 c Kylie Minogue was born in Australia.
2 b The longest river in the world is the Nile in Africa.
3 a There are five players in a basketball team.
4 b *Paella* is a Spanish dish made from rice, fish or meat and vegetables.
5 d Canberra is the capital of Australia.
6 a Alexander Graham Bell invented the telephone in 1875.
7 b The Williams sisters are Venus and Serena.
8 c George Washington was the first president of the USA.
9 d A tiger can run an amazing 56 km an hour!
10 a *Feijoada* is from Brazil. It is made from meat and beans.
11 d The Earth is 149 million km from the Sun.
12 c Golden Gate Bridge is in San Francisco.

Now count up your points!

1–4 points

Oh dear! Perhaps it's time to go to the library and read some more books!

5–7 points

Not bad but try to listen to your teacher more!

8–10 points

Well done! You know a lot of different things!

11–12 points

Congratulations! You're a general knowledge genius!

Five-minute quiz!

Answer the questions. You have only five minutes!

Pop music and films

1 Who was the star of *The Terminator*?
2 Where was the actor Antonio Banderas born?
3 Who sang the song *Hero*?

Sport

4 How many players are in a baseball team?
5 Where were the 2000 Olympic Games?
6 What sport does Martina Hingis play?

Food

7 Where does lasagne come from?
8 What is an omelette made from?
9 Where is edam cheese made?

History

10 Who was the Emperor of France from 1804 to 1815?
11 Who discovered the New World in 1492?
12 When did Martin Luther King die?

Geography

13 What is the capital of Portugal?
14 Where is the Taj Mahal?
15 What is the highest mountain in the world?

Science and nature

16 When did John Logie Baird invent the television?
17 Where can you find giraffes?
18 How many centimetres are there in a metre?

Answers

a Lisbon
b tennis
c Spain
d the Netherlands
e 100
f Enrique Iglesias
g Italy
h Arnold Schwarzenegger
i Napoleon
j 1968
k Christopher Columbus
l Mount Everest
m Sydney
n 9
o India
p 1926
q eggs
r Africa

Write your own quiz!

Write two questions for each category.

Team Name ....

Pop music and films

1 ....

....?

2 ....

....?

History

7 ....

....?

8 ....

....?

Sport

3 ....

....?

4 ....

....?

Geography

9 ....

....?

10 ....

....?

Food

5 ....

....?

6 ....

....?

Science and nature

11 ....

....?

12 ....

....?

Project 6: A famous person

Teacher's notes

Level Pre-intermediate

Language Present simple, present continuous, past simple, personal information vocabulary

Time 120 minutes

Topic Celebrities

Skills development
• Reading • Writing • Listening • Speaking

Key vocabulary actor (n), actress (n), artist (n), cycling (n), date of birth (phr), fashion design (n), favourite (adj), food (n), footballer (n), full name (n), height (n), history (n), horror film (n), library (n), nationality (n), painter (n), place of birth (phr), prince (n), princess (n), rock climbing (n), supermodel (n), tennis player (n), (TV) personality (n)

Materials
- Magazine pictures of celebrities
- Paper, coloured pens, glue, scissors

Before the lesson Photocopy:
- 1 page 31 (**Brad Pitt**) per student.
- 1 page 32 (**Venus Williams** and **Questions**) per pair of students. Cut as shown.
- 1 page 33 (**Factfile planner**) per student.

The lesson

1 Stick pictures of celebrities on the board. Ask students what they know about these people. Do they have their own favourite celebrity? Why do they like this person?

2 Tell students they are going to read a factfile about Brad Pitt. What do they know about him? Elicit ideas as a class. Note them on the board. Then give each student a photocopy of page 31 (**Brad Pitt**) and quickly go through the categories in B (*Favourite food, Hair* etc.) and check meaning. Students then match the facts in A with the categories in B. Pair check, then class feedback. Look back at the notes on the board. Were all the students' ideas correct?

3 Now tell the class they are going to read a similar factfile about Venus Williams. First give each student a photocopy of the true or false questions on page 32 (**Questions**). They predict the answers. Then give each student a photocopy of the factfile on page 32 (**Venus Williams**). They read to confirm their answers. Class feedback. Was there anything that surprised them about Venus?

4 Students now prepare to write their own factfile about a famous person of their choice. Give each student a photocopy of page 33 (**Factfile planner**). Go through the worksheet in stages as a class, elicit possible ideas and write examples on the board.

5 Give students preparation time as homework and encourage them to find out as much as possible about their celebrity. They could try to find a magazine picture of the person.

6 In class, students write a rough copy of their factfile. Encourage them to look back at the factfiles on Brad Pitt and Venus Williams for ideas. Monitor and correct their work. (You may wish to take it in to correct and do stage 7 in a later lesson.)

7 Then give students a sheet of paper on which to design and write their own factfile. Bring in coloured pens, glue and scissors. Encourage them to make it look as interesting as possible with a magazine picture of the person and small illustrations to represent their famous person's interests etc.

8 Students work in pairs and tell their partner all about their celebrity without showing the factfile. Before they start, go through the full sentences necessary to do this activity: ***His full name is*** *William Bradley Pitt.* ***He was born on*** *18th December 1963*, etc.

9 Display the factfiles on the classroom wall. Students circulate and read them. Which person did they find the most interesting?

Optional activity

Students pretend to be their famous person. Other students prepare questions and interview them. This can be done in groups or as a whole class.

Brad Pitt

Read the information about Brad Pitt.
Match the information from A to the categories from B.

	A		B
1	[d] William Bradley Pitt	a	Favourite food
2	[ ] 18th December 1963	b	Hair
3	[ ] Shawnee, Oklahoma, USA	c	Favourite sports
4	[ ] American	d	Full name
5	[ ] Actor	e	Pets
6	[ ] Jennifer (wife), Jane (mother), Bill (father), Doug (brother), Julie (sister)	f	Weight
7	[ ] 1.83 m	g	Job
8	[ ] 72 kg	h	Family
9	[ ] Blond	i	Date of birth
10	[ ] Blue	j	Favourite drink
11	[ ] Cycling, tennis, rock climbing	k	Nationality
12	[ ] Pizza	l	Eyes
13	[ ] Coffee	m	Place of birth
14	[ ] Five dogs	n	Height

Venus Williams

Full name	Venus Ebone Starr Williams
Date of birth	17th June 1980
Place of birth	Lynwood, California, USA
Nationality	American
Job	Tennis player
Family	Richard (father), Oracene (mother), Yehunde, Isha, Lyndrea and Serena (sisters)
Height	1.86 m
Weight	76 kg
Likes	Watching horror films, reading history books, learning languages
Favourite colour	Blue
Favourite country to visit	Russia
Pets	Two dogs, Starr and Pete
Ambition	To learn to speak French, Italian, German and Russian
Interesting things about Venus	She is studying fashion design at a university in Florida. She takes her dog, Pete, everywhere with her. She is interested in Russian history and Chinese culture.

Questions

Are these statements true (T) or false (F)?

1 Venus was born in California. **T / F**

2 She has three sisters. **T / F**

3 She has two dogs. **T / F**

4 Her favourite country is Italy. **T / F**

5 She would like to learn four other languages. **T / F**

6 She is studying history at university. **T / F**

Factfile planner

1 What sort of famous people are you interested in? Tick the boxes. You can tick more than one box.

- ◯ pop stars
- ◯ actors and actresses
- ◯ TV personalities
- ◯ footballers
- ◯ tennis or basketball players
- ◯ supermodels
- ◯ princes and princesses
- ◯ artists and painters

2 Write the names of three famous people that you like. Why do you like them?

Name	Reason
Brad Pitt	*He's a very good actor and he can play different roles.*
1 ______	______
2 ______	______
3 ______	______

3 Choose a person from the list above. What do you know about this person? Complete the two lists below.

Things I know	Things I don't know
______	______
______	______
______	______
______	______
______	______

4 How can you find some more information about the famous person? Tick the boxes. You can tick more than one box.

- ◯ Ask your friends.
- ◯ Ask your family.
- ◯ Look on the internet.
- ◯ Ask your teacher.
- ◯ Read magazines or newspapers.
- ◯ Read books in the library.

5 Now find out some more things about your famous person.

Project 7: The Crazy Olympics

Teacher's notes

Level Pre-intermediate

Language *Have to, can,* past simple

Time 120 minutes

Topic Unusual sports and activities

Skills development
• Reading • Writing • Listening • Speaking

Key vocabulary alarm clock (n), as (long) as possible (phr), baseball (n), basketball (n), borrow (v), careful (adj), cheerful (adj), compete (v), cup (n), dancing (n), dish washing (n), dishes (n, pl), event (n), extra point (phr), fact (n), funny (adj), glass (n), gold medal (n), golf (n), horse-riding (n), joke (n), karate (n), a long time (phr), loudly (adv), medal (n), mountain climbing (n), plate (n), quickly (adv), roller-skating (n), smile (v), snore (v), stay at home (phr), stay in bed (phr), strange (adj), take a break (phr), tell a joke (phr), tidy (adj), TV channel (n), volleyball (n), wash the dishes (phr), wash up (phr v), water-skiing (n), yachting (n)

Before the lesson Photocopy:
- 1 page 35 (**Strange but true facts about the Olympics!** and **And now the answers!**) per pair of students. Cut as shown.
- 1 page 36 per group of students. Cut into cards as shown.
- 1 page 37 (**The Crazy Olympic Games!**) per group of 4 students.

The lesson

1 Introduce the topic of the Olympic Games. Ask the class where the last Olympics were and where the next ones will be. Elicit from students their favourite events to watch and which ones they would like to enter. Brainstorm events. You could include athletics, basketball, boxing, cycling, diving, gymnastics, hockey, horse-riding, rowing, sailing, shooting, swimming. Point out that a lot of the sports end in *-ing*.

2 Tell the class that at every Olympics there are amazing stories, e.g. athletes who win large numbers of medals or competitors who are very young. Elicit such stories from the last Olympics.

3 Tell students they are going to do a quiz about strange but true Olympic facts. Quickly pre-teach/revise the following words: *baseball, borrow, climbing, compete, event, gold medal, karate, roller-skating, stolen (steal), volleyball, water-skiing, yachting.* Give each student a photocopy of **Strange but true facts about the Olympics!** on page 35 and go through the questions as a class. Tell students not to shout out the answers! In pairs, students do the quiz.

4 Give each student a photocopy of the answers (**And now the answers!**) on page 35. Go through them as a class to check any difficult words.

5 Now tell the class there is a new type of Olympic Games called the 'Crazy Olympics'. In these Olympics people compete against each other in events which involve everyday activities. Copy the first event on page 36 (*Talking on the phone)* on the board. Go through it as a class. Check the words *event* and *extra points.* Is there anybody in the class who would do well at this event?

6 Now revise the following words and phrases: *take a break, tell a joke, funny, loudly, snore, TV channel, friendly, wash the dishes, plates, cups, glasses, tidy.* Put students into groups of sixteen. (If you have a smaller number of students, you can remove some of the event cards and matching participant cards.) Explain that half the class are organising an event. Give each student in this half of the class one 'event' card from the left-hand side of page 36. The rest of the class want to participate in an event. Give this half of the class a card from the right-hand side of page 36. Ask everybody to read their cards. Remind the 'participants' that they need to use 'I' when describing themselves, e.g. *I like staying at home a lot and sitting on the sofa with my friends.*

7 Then students stand up and find the person who has a card that matches theirs. Encourage them to keep talking and moving on until they are sure they have found the right person.

8 Feedback as a class. Students read out the events and introduce the participants they have found.

9 On the board copy two of the event cards as examples. Point out the use of *-ing* for the events and *have to* for the instructions.

10 Now put students into groups of four. Tell them they are going to organise their own 'Crazy Olympics'. Give each group a photocopy of page 37 (**The Crazy Olympic Games!**) and go through the categories as a class. Students need to think of a place to have their Olympics. They also need to devise an opening and closing ceremony. Encourage them to think of past Olympics ceremonies. For example, for their opening ceremony they could have: 10,000 children sing 'The Crazy Olympic Song'. Students use their imagination and make up their own 'crazy' events with extra points for certain things.

11 One person in each group completes the worksheet. Then a representative from each group reads about their 'Crazy Olympics' to the others. Students listen and decide which 'Crazy Olympics' they would like to attend.

12 Put the sheets up on the wall for everybody to read.

Strange but true facts about the Olympics!

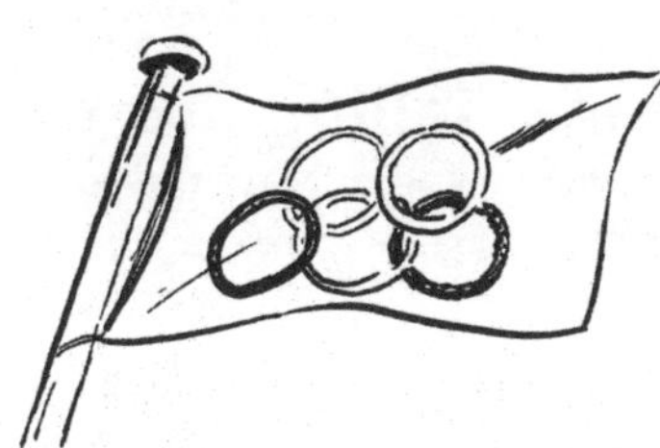

Guess the answers to the questions below...

1 In the past .... and water-skiing were Olympic events.
a dancing **b** golf **c** mountain climbing

2 Now, ... and volleyball are Olympic events.
a baseball **b** karate **c** roller-skating

3 The only Olympic events where men and women compete together are .... and yachting.
a swimming **b** basketball **c** horse-riding

4 The youngest person ever to win an Olympic gold medal was .... years old.
a seven **b** twelve **c** fourteen

5 The oldest person ever to win an Olympic medal was .... years old.
a fifty-five **b** sixty **c** seventy-two

6 At the Paris Olympic Games in 1900 the swimming events were in ....
a the River Seine **b** a lake **c** an outdoor swimming pool

7 At the Athens Olympic Games in 1896 a cyclist won a gold medal on ....
a a stolen bicycle **b** a bicycle borrowed from someone in the crowd **c** an old, broken bicycle

---

And now the answers!

1 b Golf was an Olympic event in 1900 and 1904.

2 a Baseball and volleyball are now Olympic events.

3 c Horse-riding and yachting are the only Olympic events where men and women compete against each other for medals.

4 a At the Paris Olympic Games of 1900 an unknown boy of between seven and ten won a gold medal. He sat in a boat with two rowers from Holland and helped their boat go in the right direction.

5 c The oldest person was seventy-two-year-old Oscar Swahn who won a medal in the shooting in 1920.

6 a At the Paris Olympic Games in 1900 the swimming events were in the River Seine.

7 b At the Athens Olympic Games in 1896 a cyclist won a gold medal after he borrowed a bicycle from someone in the crowd!

1 Event: Talking on the phone

You have to talk on the phone to your friends for as long as possible. You can't take any breaks.

Extra points for talking very quickly, using two mobile phones at the same time.

2 Event: Telling jokes

You have to tell as many jokes as possible in one hour. Don't forget – you mustn't laugh at your own jokes!

Extra points for very funny jokes, talking very loudly.

3 Event: Getting up late

You have to stay in bed in the morning for a very long time. You can't get out of bed at all or open your eyes.

Extra points for snoring, talking in your sleep.

4 Event: Wearing a lot of clothes

You have to wear a lot of clothes for five hours. Don't worry if you feel hot!

Extra points for putting on two pairs of jeans, wearing three hats.

5 Event: Watching television

You have to watch television for six hours. You can't move or leave the room.

Extra points for watching old films, watching the same TV channel for a very long time.

6 Event: Being cheerful

You have to be really happy and cheerful for eight hours. Don't forget to smile all the time!

Extra points for laughing a lot, being very friendly.

7 Event: Remembering songs

You have to remember all the words to a lot of different songs. You need to sing for over three hours!

Extra points for dancing, remembering very long songs.

8 Event: Dish washing

You have to wash as many plates, cups and glasses as possible in three hours. Be careful – you mustn't break any of the glasses!

Extra points for very clean dishes, singing while you are washing the cups.

a You like staying at home a lot and sitting on the sofa with your friends and family. You just love watching TV and you will watch anything!

b You are a very clean and tidy person. You love doing jobs around the house and you always wash up quickly after a meal.

c You love music and listening to your favourite songs on the radio. At home you sing and dance all the time! You would love to be a pop star.

d You often feel tired and you don't like getting out of bed in the morning. You have three different alarm clocks but your family has to wake you up every morning.

e You are a very friendly and open person. You love talking to your friends and family all the time!

f You are a very funny person. You love making all your friends laugh with your stories and jokes!

g You often feel very cold and you like wearing a big jacket and warm boots in the winter. You would like to live in a very hot country.

h You are a very happy person. You can't stop smiling and laughing. When you wake up every morning, you jump out of bed with a big smile on your face!

The Crazy Olympic Games!

Come to the craziest Olympics ever!

Place ....

Year ....

Opening ceremony ....

....

Main event 1 ....

Extra points ....

Main event 2 ....

Extra points ....

Main event 3 ....

Extra points ....

Closing ceremony ....

....

Tickets cost

....

Organisers

....

Project 8: My own restaurant

Teacher's notes

Level Pre-intermediate

Language Requests, ordering food, food vocabulary

Time 150 minutes

Topic Food and restaurants

Skills development
• Reading • Writing • Listening • Speaking

Key vocabulary Austrian (adj), barbecued (adj), bun (n), butter (n), Chinese (adj), cream (n), delicious (adj), flour (n), green bean (n), green pepper (n), ham (n), ice cream sundae (n), Indian (adj), lettuce (n), list (n), rice (n), main course (n), meat (n), Mexican (adj), milkshake (n), mushroom (n), onion (n), pineapple (n), prawn (n), serve (with) (v), sparkling (adj), steak (n), still (adj), sugar (n), today's special (phr)

Materials
- Pictures of food from magazines or recipe books
- Coloured pens, paper

Before the lesson Photocopy:
- 1 page 39 per group of 6 students. Cut into cards as shown.
- 1 page 40 per group of 6 students. Cut into cards as shown.
- 1 page 41 (**Heavy Rock Café**) per pair of students.

The lesson

1 Introduce the topic of food and restaurants. Ask students about their favourite food. Show pictures of different types of food (pizza, salad etc.) from recipe books or magazines to generate interest and revise vocabulary.

2 Pre-teach/revise the following words and check if they are countable/uncountable: *butter, cream, flour, green bean, green pepper, ham, ice cream sundae, meat, mushroom, onion, pancake, pineapple, prawn, rice, sugar.* Ask students what type of food they like from different countries. Aim to elicit *Italian, Chinese, American, Mexican, Indian* and *Austrian* (think of the cakes!).

3 Now organise the game on pages 39 and 40. Tell students they run a restaurant in a busy street with lots of other international restaurants. They are cooking today's special dish at their restaurant but they have run out of some ingredients. They need to look at their list and ask the other restaurant owners for the missing ingredients.

4 First give each student a photocopy of a restaurant card on page 39. Ask them to read it and help with vocabulary if necessary. Students play the game in groups of six or as a class. If you have more than multiples of six, give out extra cards; the game will still work.

5 Then give each student a photocopy of an ingredient card from page 40 so they now have two cards. Students must have the same number restaurant and ingredient card, e.g. number 4 from page 39 and number 4 from page 40.

6 Revise quickly requests and replies such as: *Have you got any cheese/tomatoes? Yes, I have./No, sorry, I haven't.*

7 Students move around the room and ask each other for the ingredients on their restaurant card (i.e. the ingredients they need to make today's special). When they are given an ingredient, they tick it off on their restaurant card; the person who gives them the ingredient must put a cross through the relevant picture on their ingredients card. The food item can only be given away once. Students can only ask a person for one thing at a time; they then need to move on. They can come back to a student after they have talked to some others.

8 The winner is the first student who finds all the ingredients for their today's special.

9 Now give each pair of students a photocopy of the menu on page 41 (**Heavy Rock Café**). Go through the menu as a class. Check any unknown vocabulary. Students write down what they would choose for a meal at this restaurant and guess what their partner would choose.

10 Students then prepare for a role play in pairs using the menu. One person is a waiter, the other is a customer. As a class, go through useful waiter expressions such as: *Would you like a table for one/two? Are you ready to order? Can I get you anything to drink? Here's your … . Would you like a dessert?* Then focus on customer expressions: *Yes, I'd like the …, please. I'll have the …, please. Can I have the bill, please?* Students do the role play and order food they would like from the menu. Then they reverse roles. At the end, students see if their predictions about their partner's choice of food were correct.

11 Now, in pairs, students imagine they have their own restaurant. It could have food from a certain country or a special theme. They plan, write and design an attractive menu for it. Monitor and help with vocabulary /expressions etc. Ask them to do a rough draft first and correct it. Then give out coloured pens, paper etc. and get them to create a final version.

12 Each pair then sets up their own small 'restaurant' in class. They invite other pairs into the restaurant to choose from the menu and have a meal. Students use the waiter/customer expressions from the previous role play. As class feedback, students can give their impressions of the restaurants they visited.

1 LA PIAZZA

(Italian restaurant)

Today's special:
Ham and mushroom pizza

- ☐ cheese
- ☐ ham
- ☐ tomatoes
- ☐ mushrooms
- ☐ a green pepper
- ☐ an onion
- ☐ flour

2 San Francisco Diner

(American restaurant)

Today's special:
Hawaiian ice cream sundae

- ☐ ice cream
- ☐ cream
- ☐ sugar
- ☐ chocolate
- ☐ strawberries
- ☐ bananas
- ☐ pineapple

3 El Mexicano

(Mexican café)

Today's special:
Mexican pancakes

- ☐ flour
- ☐ eggs
- ☐ milk
- ☐ meat
- ☐ tomatoes
- ☐ carrots
- ☐ cheese

4 China Garden

(Chinese restaurant)

Today's special:
Prawns with vegetables and rice

- ☐ rice
- ☐ prawns
- ☐ a green pepper
- ☐ mushrooms
- ☐ carrots
- ☐ green beans
- ☐ an onion

5 Bombay Palace

(Indian restaurant)

Today's special:
Curry with rice

- ☐ rice
- ☐ meat
- ☐ an onion
- ☐ tomatoes
- ☐ carrots
- ☐ a green pepper
- ☐ green beans

6 Vienna House

(Austrian café)

Today's special:
Chocolate and cream cake

- ☐ flour
- ☐ chocolate
- ☐ butter
- ☐ eggs
- ☐ milk
- ☐ sugar
- ☐ cream

1 In your restaurant you've got …

2 In your restaurant you've got …

3 In your restaurant you've got …

4 In your restaurant you've got …

5 In your restaurant you've got …

6 In your restaurant you've got …

Heavy Rock Café

The coolest, loudest restaurant in town with food that everybody loves!

Main courses

New York Pizza
Our biggest ever pizza with mushrooms, green pepper, tomatoes and lots of cheese!

Hawaiian Burger
Your favourite burger in a bun with delicious pineapple.

Barbecued Cheeseburger
The best burger in town! A large barbecued burger in a bun with cheese.

Chinese Chicken Salad
A salad with tomatoes, green pepper, lettuce and our famous Chinese chicken.

Texas Steak
An old favourite! A large steak served with chips and salad.

Fish Cakes
Two big fish cakes served with green salad and new potatoes.

Desserts

Italian Ice Cream Sundae
Chocolate, vanilla and strawberry ice cream with fresh cream. It's fantastic!

Chocolate Fudge Brownie
Our famous American chocolate cake served with ice cream.

Banana Split
Vanilla ice cream with bananas and lots of cream. Try it!

Strawberry Cheesecake
American cheesecake with strawberries and cream. Delicious!

Fruit Salad
Bananas, strawberries, pineapple and much more! Served with ice cream.

Drinks

Milkshakes
Strawberry, chocolate or banana.
Try our milkshakes. You'll want another one!

Coke

Lemonade

Orange juice

Mineral water
Still or sparkling.

Coffee

Project 9: Where I live

Teacher's notes

Level Pre-intermediate

Language Directions, present simple, places in a town

Time 240 minutes

Topic Giving directions, describing a town

Skills development
• Reading • Writing • Listening • Speaking

Key vocabulary
ancient (adj), antique (n), bridge (n), camping site (n), castle (n), cosmopolitan (adj), discover (v), dungeon (n), farm (n), ghost (n), haunted (adj), historic (adj), hospital (n), leaflet (n), library (n), museum (n), narrow (adj), picturesque (adj), post office (n), rich (adj), river (n), second-hand (adj), visitor attraction (n), watch out (phr v)

Materials
- A town map
- Coloured pens, glue, scissors
- Town guides/leaflets from the local tourist office (optional)

Before the lesson Photocopy:
- 1 page 43 (**A map of Bridgetown**) per student.
- 1 page 44 (**Welcome to Bridgetown**) per pair of students.
- 1 **Questions** on page 45 per pair of students.
- 1 **Leaflet planner** on page 45 per pair of students.

The lesson

1 Bring in a map of the town where you live. Point to some key places, e.g. station, hospital etc. and ask students if they know what these places are in English.

2 Give each student a photocopy of page 43 (**A map of Bridgetown**). Go through the places that are already written on the map: *post office, police station* etc. Then check the meaning of the places in the box. Look at the first example together as a class. Students write in the rest of the missing places on their own, then check in pairs. Class feedback.

3 Now use the map to practise giving and following directions. Pre-teach/revise the following expressions: *Turn left/right (at the post office). Take the first/second turning on the left/right. Go straight on. Go over the bridge. Go over the crossroads. It's in front of you/on your left/right. It's near the park. You can't miss it!*

4 Choose a place on the map, e.g. the school or hospital. Don't tell the students what it is. Give detailed directions to that place and see if the students can find the final destination. Tell them to start at the cross on the map and follow your directions carefully. Ask two or three stronger students to do the same in turns in front of the whole class.

5 Students now do the same activity in pairs. One student gives directions to a mystery place on the map to their partner. The other student follows the directions to see where they lead. Students then swap roles. Listen and make notes of errors. Go through these on the board at the end.

6 Tell students they are now going to read a tourist leaflet about the same town. Quickly pre-teach the following words: *ancient, dungeon, ghost, haunted, historic, narrow, picturesque, second-hand, watch out.* Give each pair of students a photocopy of page 44 (**Welcome to Bridgetown**). Get them to read the first 'page' quickly and tell you what is special about Bridgetown. (It is the most haunted town in Britain.)

7 Ask students to read the rest of the leaflet quickly and find the names of three famous ghosts in the town (the Singing Ghost, the Lady in White and the Horse and Rider). Class feedback.

8 Now give each student a photocopy of the **Questions** on page 45. Quickly revise the following question words: *how long, when, what, where, how far* and *which*. Students answer questions in pairs. The exercise can be done as a race. Class feedback.

9 Quickly go through the structure of the leaflet on page 44 (**Welcome to Bridgetown**) and point out the introduction and the various sections ('Places to visit', etc.).

10 In pairs, students now plan a leaflet of their city, town or village. (This could alternatively be the capital city or another interesting town they know.) Give each pair of students a photocopy of the **Leaflet planner** on page 45. Go through the vocabulary as a class and help students with ideas for other special places to visit. Encourage students to refer back to the Bridgetown leaflet for useful expressions etc.

11 Students write a rough draft of their own leaflet as class work or homework. Provide correction on this. Bring in coloured pens, glue, scissors and town guides/leaflets from your local tourist office if possible. Students then produce their own final leaflet with illustrations or pictures from the guides/leaflets.

12 Put the students' leaflets on a wall display. Students circulate and read. They decide which leaflet makes the city, town or village sound the most interesting for visitors.

A map of Bridgetown

Look at the map of Bridgetown. Write the places in the boxes on the map.

bridge ~~café~~ castle cinema hospital park river school station supermarket

8 ....

10 ....

SAVERS

9 ....

museum

7 ....

library

bank

6 ....

5 ....

3 ....

4 ....

police station

post office

POST OFFICE

2 ....

1 ....café..........

WELCOME TO BRIDGETOWN

Only 40 minutes by train from London

Come to the most haunted town in Britain! Walk along the ancient narrow streets and discover hundreds of historic buildings. Don't forget to watch out for the ghosts!

Places to visit

Bridgetown is rich in history, with many interesting visitor attractions.

The Castle

Come and find out about the horror of the past! Visit the famous castle dungeons and listen carefully for the Singing Ghost. Don't forget to go home!

The North Bridge

Built in 1489, the North Bridge is one of the oldest and most picturesque bridges in England. You can get a good view of the town from here.

The Old Market

Come on a Saturday and visit one of the best second-hand markets in Europe. Buy fantastic clothes, CDs, pictures and antiques.

Places to stay

The Old Lion Hotel ★★★★★

The hotel is a sixteenth century building with excellent facilities. Stay in the haunted bedroom and look for the ghost of the Lady in White!

The Olympia Hotel ★★★★★

A modern hotel for people who love sport. Try out the new gym, swimming pool and sauna. Stay here and get fit. No ghosts here!

Sunny Farm Camping Site

Bring your tent and stay at this beautiful farm one kilometre outside the town. On a dark night you can see the famous ghost of the Horse and Rider.

How to get there

By road: Take the M23 south of London and turn off on the B216 to Bridgetown.

By train: There are frequent trains from London Victoria station.

Questions

1 How long is it by train from London to Bridgetown?
2 What is the castle famous for?
3 When was the North Bridge built?
4 When can you find a market in Bridgetown?
5 What can you buy at the market?
6 Where is the ghost of The Lady in White?
7 Where can you stay if you like sport?
8 How far is Sunny Farm Camping Site from the town?
9 Which two roads can you take to Bridgetown?
10 Which London station can you take the train from?

Leaflet planner

Name of town ....

Population ....

Location

Our town is in the north / south / east / west / centre of our country.

Special things about our town

- [ ] old
- [ ] picturesque
- [ ] romantic
- [ ] cosmopolitan
- [ ] warm in the summer
- [ ] interesting shops
- [ ] good sports facilities
- [ ] lively night life
- [ ] lots of different restaurants and cafés

Other things ....

Places to visit in our town

- [ ] museum
- [ ] swimming pool
- [ ] theatre
- [ ] park
- [ ] art gallery
- [ ] famous shops
- [ ] castle
- [ ] cinema
- [ ] beach
- [ ] market

Other places ....

How to get to our town

By road ....

By bus ....

By train ....

Where to stay

1 ....

2 ....

3 ....

Project 10: Aliens from outer space!

Teacher's notes

Level Pre-intermediate

Language Present simple, past simple

Time 120 minutes

Topic Aliens from outer space

Skills development
• Reading • Writing • Listening • Speaking

Key vocabulary afraid (adj), alien (n), army (n), asteroid (n), body (n), destroy (v), disappear (v), entertainment (n), expert (n), human form (phr), island (n), islander (n), land (v), leader (n), the Moon (n), outer space (n), Planet Earth (n), South Pacific Ocean (n), space ship (n), strange (adj), UFO (n)

Materials Sheets of paper

Before the lesson Photocopy:
- 1 page 47 (**Aliens from outer space!** and **Questions**) per student (or pair of students). Cut as shown.
- 1 **Find the aliens** on page 48 per group of 10 students. Cut into cards as shown.
- 1 **Message** on page 48 per pair of students.
- 1 page 49 (**Help the Zenons from Planet Zog!**) per group of 4 students.

The lesson

1 Ask students if they have seen any films about UFOs or aliens. What happened in the films? Establish the following words: *UFO* (pronounced as separate letters, U-F-O), *alien, space ship* and *outer space*. Do they believe in UFOs and aliens?

2 Tell the class they are going to read a newspaper article entitled **Aliens from Outer Space!** Pre-teach/revise the following words and phrases: *army, body, disappear, expert, human form, island, islander, (to) land, (the) Moon, Planet Earth, South Pacific Ocean, strange*.

3 Give each student (or pair of students) a photocopy of the **Questions** on page 47. Go through them with students.

4 Then give each student (or pair of students) a photocopy of **Aliens from Outer Space!** on page 47. Tell students to read it quickly and answer the questions. Pair check, then class check. Elicit from students what the UFO expert says. (Friends and family may have become aliens.)

5 Now tell students that they are going to play a game called 'Find the aliens'. Some people in the class have been taken over by the aliens from Planet Zog. These aliens can copy human behaviour but they may make some mistakes. Students find out who the aliens are by asking everybody in the room what they did yesterday.

6 On the board write: *What did you do yesterday?* Then write these phrases on the board: *play tennis, watch TV, have lunch with a friend*. Get students to make sentences: *I played tennis, I watched TV, I had lunch with a friend*. Quickly go through the meaning and pronunciation of these past forms: *cooked, had (lunch/dinner etc.), listened, met, read, talked, visited, went*.

7 Students work in groups of ten or fewer. Give each student a card from the **Find the aliens** game on page 48. Take out some of the *You are not an alien* cards if you have fewer than ten students in a group. Ensure that students understand if they are/aren't aliens by going through *You are an alien* and *You are <u>not</u> an alien* on the board. Students must keep their identity secret. Don't reveal how many aliens there are (two per group).

8 Students move around their group asking each other: *What did you do yesterday?* Each student must use all the phrases on their card but not add any more information. The student who asked the question must listen carefully for any slightly strange replies. For example, one of the aliens *talked to a dog* and *looked at the moon all night*. Students mustn't say anything if they find an alien, they must move on to another person.

9 When the class has finished, ask everybody to guess who the aliens were. What clues were there? The aliens now reveal themselves.

10 Pre-teach the following words: *afraid, asteroid, destroy, entertainment, leader*. Now ask the alien students to give each pair of students a photocopy of the **Message** on page 48. Ask students to read the message and find the answers to these questions: *What happened to Planet Zog ten years ago? What problem do the Zenons have now? How can you help the Zenons?*

11 Go through the answers to the questions. Tell the class to help the Zenons by choosing the best things from Planet Earth to send back in a space ship to Planet Zog.

12 Go through the categories of the worksheet on page 49 (**Help the Zenons from Planet Zog!**) and elicit ideas for each. For example, in the *Inventions* section these could be the telephone, the TV, the computer etc. In the *Photos and biography of a famous person* section, students stick a photo of a famous person and write a brief biography on a separate sheet to inspire the Zenons; it could be someone like Martin Luther King, Mahatma Gandhi or even a footballer like David Beckham.

13 Put students in groups of four and give each group a photocopy of page 49 (**Help the Zenons from Planet Zog!**). They discuss and record their ideas. Monitor and help with vocabulary. Encourage the use of English.

14 Students make poster presentations of the things they have chosen to send to Planet Zog. They could illustrate their ideas with pictures, photos from magazines etc. Put the posters on the classroom wall for everybody to read. As feedback, discuss who chose the best group of things to help the Zenons rebuild their world.

The Daily News 4th March

Aliens from Outer Space!

Yesterday thousands of UFOs appeared in the sky above the island of Vanutu in the South Pacific Ocean. Islanders phoned friends in Australia and the UK to say that strange space ships were landing near their houses. One man saw twenty aliens climbing out of the largest space ship. 'It was very dark but I could see that they were small with large round faces and three eyes.'

Soldiers from the Australian army landed on the island of Vanutu last night. They found thousands of small space ships everywhere. 'We walked up to some of the space ships,' said Captain Chris Smith. 'But when we looked inside, they were empty. The aliens have all disappeared. It's very strange.'

UFO expert Professor Paul Johnston arrived on the island late last night. 'I'm sure the aliens are still on Planet Earth,' he said. 'I think these beings might be Zenons from Planet Zog. It's possible that they will enter our bodies and take the human form. Over the next five days, people all over the world must be very careful. Look at your friends and family. Have they become an alien? Perhaps they will start to do strange things. Children may start to tidy their bedrooms, students will ask for more homework. Watch out! These could be the signs of an alien from outer space!'

Questions

Choose the best answer.

1. The space ships landed ....
   a in Australia **b** in the South Pacific Ocean **c** on the island of Vanutu
2. The aliens had ....
   a small faces and big eyes **b** big faces and three eyes **c** three faces and large eyes
3. When Captain Chris Smith looked inside the space ships, ...
   a he didn't see any aliens **b** he saw twenty aliens **c** he saw thousands of aliens
4. Professor Paul Johnston says the aliens are now ....
   a in space **b** on Planet Earth **c** on the Moon
5. Professor Johnston thinks the aliens now look like ....
   a people **b** animals **c** cars

Find the aliens

1 You are not an alien!
Yesterday you did these things:
have breakfast, play tennis, have lunch with friends, read a book, listen to some CDs, cook dinner, watch TV

2 You are not an alien!
Yesterday you did these things:
have breakfast, go swimming, have lunch at a café, visit a friend, read a magazine, have dinner at home, listen to the radio

3 You are not an alien!
Yesterday you did these things: have breakfast, play basketball, have lunch at home, phone a friend, have dinner at a friend's house, play computer games, watch TV

4 You are not an alien!
Yesterday you did these things:
have breakfast, go running, have lunch at a restaurant, watch a film on TV, play tennis, have dinner at home, listen to some CDs

5 You are not an alien!
Yesterday you did these things: have breakfast, read a magazine, go to a fast food restaurant for lunch, watch tennis on TV, read a book, have dinner with a friend, go swimming

6 You are not an alien!
Yesterday you did these things:
have coffee, go shopping, have lunch, watch sport on TV, have dinner at home, go to the cinema, meet some friends, read the newspaper

7 You are not an alien!
Yesterday you did these things:
have breakfast, listen to the radio, read a book, have lunch at home, go running, play computer games, have dinner with a friend

8 You are not an alien!
Yesterday you did these things: have breakfast, read the newspaper, have lunch with a friend, go shopping, play tennis, have dinner at a restaurant, watch an old film on TV

9 You are an alien!
Yesterday you did these things:
have breakfast, talk to a dog, work on the computer, have lunch, listen to the radio, have dinner, look at the Moon all night

10 You are an alien!
Yesterday you did these things:
have breakfast, clean the television, have lunch, go shopping, take a lot of photos, watch the radio, have dinner at a restaurant

Message

Dear Human,

Do not be afraid! We are Zenons from Planet Zog. Ten years ago a large asteroid hit our planet. It destroyed all of our houses, cities and beautiful buildings. We have a terrible life now – we don't have any good food, sport or entertainment. Please tell us about the best things from Planet Earth and help us to start a new life on Planet Zog.

Thank you,
Zig
Leader of the Zenons

Help the Zenons from Planet Zog!

Choose the best things from Planet Earth to help the Zenons rebuild life on Planet Zog.

The best everyday inventions

1 ....
2 ....
3 ....

The best means of transport

1 ....
2 ....
3 ....

Photos of a famous building

Photos and maps of a beautiful city

The best food

1 ....
2 ....
3 ....

The most interesting sports or activities

1 ....
2 ....
3 ....

The best CDs

1 ....
2 ....
3 ....

The best films

1 ....
2 ....
3 ....

The best books

1 ....
2 ....
3 ....

Photos and biography of a famous person

Project 11: A new theme park

Teacher's notes

Level Pre-intermediate

Language Present simple, *there is/are*, adjectives to describe places

Time 150 minutes

Topic Theme parks

Skills development
• Reading • Writing

Key vocabulary advances (n, pl), amazing (adj), Christmas (n), factory (n), journey (n), light (n), magic show (phr), ride (n), popular (adj), product (n), story (n), theme park (n), place (n), visitor (n), (visitor) attraction (n)

Materials
- Coloured pens, paper, blu-tack or drawing pins
- Atlas (optional)

Before the lesson Photocopy:
- 3 page 51. Cut as shown. (With a small class, 1 or 2 photocopies will be enough.)
- 1 page 52 (**Three theme parks**) per pair of students.
- 1 page 53 (**A new theme park**) per group of 4 students.

The lesson

1 Introduce the word *theme park*. Elicit from the class the names of any theme parks they know and what people can do there. Aim to establish the following words: *visitor attraction, ride, show, visitor*.

2 Tell students they are going to read about three different theme parks. Write the names of these theme parks on the board: *Santa's Enchanted Forest, Futuroscope* and *Cadbury World*. See if they can guess what the themes of these places are. They will need some clues, especially with the last one. Tell students that Cadbury's make something you can eat. (Cadbury's make confectionary and are especially famous for their chocolate.)

3 Pre-teach/revise the following words: *advances* (as in 'the latest advances in film/computers'), *amazing, Christmas, factory, journey, light (n), magic show, popular, product, story.*

4 Put the photocopies of the texts on page 51 on the classroom wall. Make sure there are plenty of copies so that all students can read about the different theme parks without waiting too long to have access to the texts.

5 Give each pair of students a photocopy of page 52 (**Three theme parks**). Go through the worksheet as a class and ensure students know what type of information to put in each space. Students then stand up, circulate around the class, read the three different texts about the theme parks and complete the information. Go through the answers as a class. Students say which theme park they would like to visit and why. If you have an atlas, you can find where the different places are situated.

6 Now put students into groups of four. Explain that they are going to develop their own theme park. Remind them of the themes of the theme parks they have read about (chocolate, the science and technology of the future, Christmas). Tell them to brainstorm ideas for five minutes and then choose one main theme. Circulate and help them with the English words to describe their theme.

7 Give each group of students a photocopy of page 53 (**A new theme park**). As a class, go through the categories and briefly brainstorm what students could write in each space.

8 In groups, students discuss and develop their own theme park. Circulate, encourage the use of English and help with unknown words. Students could use bilingual dictionaries if they want to.

9 Take in and correct their worksheets.

10 In a subsequent lesson, students can make posters using simple English to advertise their theme park. Bring in coloured pens and paper for the posters. Encourage students to put a slogan at the top of their advertisement, e.g. *Visit … theme park!* and include some of the sentences from their theme park planner (**A new theme park**) in a short text at the bottom. As a class, you could quickly design the layout of a poster on the board as a model and show where to put the slogan, illustrations and short text.

11 Put the posters up on the classroom wall. Students can choose which theme park they would like to visit.

If you love chocolate, visit **Cadbury World** in Birmingham, UK. This popular visitor attraction tells you all about chocolate and how it is made. Go on a magical chocolate journey and visit the children's chocolate factory! There is also a theatre and an exciting video story.

At **Cadbury World** you can buy hundreds of chocolate products in the shop and café. Have fun but don't eat too much!

Over 500,000 people visit **Cadbury World** every year. It is open from 9 am to 5 pm every day between March and October. It is closed on some days between November and February.

Santa's Enchanted Forest is the world's biggest Christmas theme park with over 400,000 visitors every year. There are hundreds of 'Christmas' things to do for all the family. You can meet Father Christmas and have your photo taken with him. There is also one of the tallest Christmas trees in the world with over 70,000 lights!

Santa's Enchanted Forest has rides, magic shows and different types of Christmas food and drink. Don't forget, all of this comes with wonderful Christmas music!

Santa's Enchanted Forest is near Miami in the United States. It is open from the beginning of November until January. You can go from 5 pm to midnight every day.

Futuroscope is a science theme park near Poitiers in France. Over 3 million people travel here each year to discover the latest advances in film, video, computers and the internet. Both parents and children will enjoy this amazing place.

There are more than 70 different attractions which include giant 3D cinemas and exciting rides. **Futuroscope** is very big and covers over 53 hectares! Stay in one of the hotels inside the park and visit for two or three days. You can go to **Futuroscope** all year round. It is usually open from 9 am to 6 pm.

Three theme parks

Read the information about the three different theme parks.
Complete the table below.

	Cadbury World	Santa's Enchanted Forest	Futuroscope
Theme			Science and technology of the future.
City	Birmingham		
Country		the USA	
Open	March to October, 9 am to 5 pm. Closed some days from November to February.		
Number of visitors			Over 3 million people every year.
Things to do and see	The children's chocolate factory, the magical chocolate journey, theatre, video story, shop and café.		

A new theme park

Name of theme park

The theme park is called ....

Place (town and country)

It is in ....

Theme

The theme park is all about ....

....

Attractions, rides and things to do

You can ....

....

Shops

You can buy ....

....

Restaurants and cafés

You can eat ....

Hotels

You can stay at ....

Transport

You can get there by ....

Open

You can visit the theme park .... (months)

It is open from .... (time)

Price

It costs .... for adults and .... for children.

Project 12: A new pop group

Teacher's notes

Level Intermediate

Language Present simple, pop music vocabulary

Time 150 minutes

Topic Pop music

Skills development
• Reading • Writing • Listening • Speaking

Key vocabulary album (n), award (n), bass guitar (n), ceremony (n), charts (n, pl), contract (n), drums (n, pl), fan (n), keyboards (n, pl), lead guitar (n), lead singer (n), lyrics (n, pl), pop group (n), record company (n), saxophone (n), single (n), soundtrack (n), tour (n), trumpet (n)

Materials
- 1 dice per group of 5 students, 1 counter for each student
- Pictures of pop stars (optional)

Before the lesson Photocopy:
- 1 page 55 (**Vocabulary**) per pair of students.
- 1 board for the game on pages 56 and 57 (**Game: You're a pop star!**) per group of 3–6 students. Cut and stick the pages together as shown.
- 1 set of cards on pages 58 and 59 per group of 3–6 students.
- 1 **Our pop group** on page 59 per group of 4–5 students.

The lesson

1 Bring in some pictures of pop stars. Alternatively, ask students to bring in pictures of their favourite stars plus CDs/tapes of their music if possible. Encourage a class discussion about the types of music they prefer (keep it light-hearted). Aim to elicit some of the following musical genres: *disco, folk, house, jazz, heavy metal, rap, rock and roll, soul, techno.*

2 Give each pair of students a photocopy of page 55 (**Vocabulary**). Tell the class the words will be useful for a board game about pop music they will play later. In pairs, students match words and definitions. Monitor and help. Go through the answers as a class. Check the meaning and pronunciation of the words.

3 As a class, quickly go through the game-playing expressions at the end of this book (**Glossary of useful expressions, Playing a game**, page 94).

4 Put the class into groups of between three and six around a table. Give each group a board for the game (**Game: You're a pop star!**), a full set of cards from pages 58 and 59 and a dice. Then give each student a counter. Ask students to put a corresponding 'Good luck!' and 'Bad luck!' card face down on each 'Chance' square on the board. For example, the pair of 'Good luck!' and 'Bad luck!' cards with 'A' at the top go on the 'Chance A' square, the pair of 'Good luck!' and 'Bad luck!' cards with 'B' at the top go on the 'Chance B' square, and so on. Ask students not to read the cards yet.

5 Tell students the rules for the game:
- The background to the game is that each player is a solo pop singer who plays the guitar. All their friends say they have a fantastic voice and they write wonderful songs. They decide to become rich and famous in the world of pop.
- The first person throws the dice and moves their counter the correct number of spaces. The students take it in turns to throw the dice and move their counters.
- If a person lands on a 'Chance' square, they must throw the dice again. If they throw a number from one to three, they read the 'Bad luck!' card out loud to the others. If they throw four to six, they read the 'Good luck!' card out loud. They must then move back or forward two spaces or four spaces as indicated.
- If a person lands on a square with an arrow, they must move to the space indicated.
- The aim of the game is to be the first person to reach the number one spot in the music charts.

6 When the game is finished, tell the class they are going to form their own pop groups. They will be the members of the band. Put the students in groups of four or five. Give each group a photocopy of **Our pop group** on page 59. Go through the categories as a class and elicit possible ideas. The instruments might include the following: *bass guitar, drums, keyboards, lead guitar, saxophone, trumpet.* Encourage each student to make up their own names such as *Big Bob on the drums* or *Crazy Chris as lead singer.*

7 Then students work in their groups. One person records the ideas on the worksheet. When students have finished they can present their group to the class. This could alternatively be done as a poster presentation.

Optional activity

At the end, students could also do a role play of an interview between a journalist and a member of the band. Half the class are journalists and prepare questions for the pop stars. They then conduct the interview and swap roles.

Vocabulary

Here are some words about the world of pop music.
Match the words in A to the definitions in B.

A		B
1 ☐ a fan	a	the words of a song
2 ☐ a single	b	the music from a film
3 ☐ an album	c	a business that produces and sells CDs and cassettes
4 ☐ the lyrics	d	a short CD or cassette with only one song on it
5 ☐ a soundtrack	e	a person who likes a pop group very much
6 ☐ the charts	f	a prize for a person who has done something very well
7 ☐ a record company	g	a legal agreement between people, usually in writing
8 ☐ a contract	h	a list of the forty most popular songs in a particular week
9 ☐ a tour	i	a CD or cassette with a lot of different songs on it
10 ☐ an award	j	a journey to many different towns where a musician gives concerts

Game: You're

You are Number 1!

1	2	3 Fans follow you everywhere. You have to stay at home.	4 **Chance M**
16 **Chance I**	15	14 **Chance J**	13
17	18	19 Someone steals your favourite guitar.	20 **Chance H**
32 **Chance C**	31	30	29 You have a bad cold and you can't sing.
33	34 **Chance B**	35	36

a pop star!

5	6	7	8 Chance L
12	11 You have an argument with your manager.	10 Chance K	9

21	22 Chance G	23	24 Chance F
28 Chance D	27	26 Chance E	25

37	38 Chance A	39	40 Start Here

A Good luck!
You're playing the guitar in the street. The manager of a record company sees you. He gives you his phone number.
» 2 spaces

B Good luck!
It's your first concert today! Five hundred people come.
» 4 spaces

C Good luck!
You have your first recording contract with a big record company.
» 2 spaces

D Good luck!
You make your first single. It's played on the radio every day.
» 4 spaces

E Good luck!
Your first single goes into the charts at number 25.
» 2 spaces

F Good luck!
You make your first album. Everybody loves it! You sell 1 million albums in the first month.
» 4 spaces

G Good luck!
You do a tour of Europe. Millions of fans see you in concert.
» 2 spaces

H Good luck!
You go on television three times in one week. You look very good in your new clothes.
» 2 spaces

I Good luck!
Your second single goes into the charts at number 4.
» 2 spaces

J Good luck!
You are invited to perform at an international music festival. Everybody wants to meet you.
» 2 spaces

K Good Luck!
You do a big tour of the USA. You give a concert for the US president.
» 2 points

L Good luck!
You are now very famous. Your photo is on the front page of all the magazines.
» 2 spaces

M Good luck!
You do the soundtrack for a Hollywood film. You make a lot of money and buy a holiday home in Florida.
» 2 spaces

A Bad luck!
You're playing the guitar in the street. The manager of a record company sees you. He gives you his phone number but you lose it.
« 2 spaces

B Bad luck!
It's your first concert today! Only twenty people come.
« 4 spaces

C Bad luck!
You visit a lot of record companies. Nobody wants to talk to you.
« 2 spaces

D Bad luck!
You make your first single. It's never played on the radio.
« 4 spaces

E Bad luck!
Your first single doesn't go into the charts.
« 2 spaces

F Bad luck!
You make your first album. You only sell 100 copies in the first week.
« 4 spaces

G Bad luck!
You start to do a tour of Europe but you become ill. You go home.
« 2 spaces

H Bad luck!
You go on television but you fall over. Everybody laughs at you.
« 2 spaces

I Bad luck!
Your second single only goes into the charts at number 40.
« 2 spaces

J Bad luck!
You want to sing at an international music festival but you aren't invited to perform. You watch the festival at home on TV.
« 4 spaces

K Bad luck!
You do a concert in New York. You forget some of the lyrics to your songs.
« 2 spaces

L Bad luck!
You drive too fast and the police stop you. You go to prison for a week. You are on the front page of all the newspapers.
« 4 spaces

M Bad luck!
You have an argument with your record company. You have to pay them a lot of money.
« 2 spaces

Our pop group

Name of the group ....

Type of music ....

Type of clothes ....

Number of people ....

Names of the people in the band and their instrument

1 ....

2 ....

3 ....

4 ....

5 ....

Name of our first single ....

Name of our first album ....

First concert (place and number of fans) ....

....

Future plans ....

....

Project 13: A better zoo

Teacher's notes

Level Intermediate

Language Present simple, *have got*, future tenses, animal vocabulary

Time 240 minutes

Topic Animals and zoos

Skills development
• Reading • Writing • Listening • Speaking

Key vocabulary bear (n), camel (n), century (n), conservation (n), crocodile (n), cruel (adj), deer (n), demonstration (n), dolphin (n), donkey (n), in doubt (phr), drop (v), eagle (n), elephant (n), fall into decline (phr), giraffe (n), goat (n), gorilla (n), habitat (n), height (n), hoof (n), leopard (n), lion (n), lifespan (n), male (adj), monkey (n), owl (n), panda (n), parrot (n), penguin (n), rabbit (n), in need of repair (phr), resident (n), seal (n), speed (n), species (n), tiger (n), weight (n), whale (n), zebra (n)

Materials
- Coloured pens
- Reference books on animals (optional)

Before the lesson Photocopy:
- 1 page 61 (**Animal crossword: Student A**) for all students designated Student A.
- 1 page 62 (**Animal crossword: Student B**) for all students designated Student B.
- 1 page 63 per pair of students (**Uncertain future for town zoo**, **Questions** and **Opinions**). Cut as shown.
- 1 **Zoo budget** on page 64 per group of 4–6 students.
- 1 **Giraffe factfile** on page 64 per pair of students (optional).
- 1 page 65 (**Plan of the zoo**) per group of 4–6 students. Enlarge if possible.

The lesson

1 Students brainstorm zoo animals. Go through the words on the board. Try to cover the vocabulary on pages 61 and 62 (**Animal crossword: Student A** and **Animal crossword: Student B**): *bear, camel, crocodile, deer, dolphin, eagle, elephant, giraffe, gorilla, leopard, lion, monkey, owl, panda, parrot, penguin, seal, tiger, zebra, whale.*

2 Elicit descriptions of two of the animals using the following phrases: *It's got (four) legs. It lives in (Africa). It's (brown/black and white). It's got (spots/stripes). It's got (a long neck/trunk). It lives (in water/on land). It is/isn't (fierce). It's similar to a (lion).*

3 Divide the class into two groups, A and B. Give each student in group A a photocopy of page 61 (**Animal crossword: Student A**). Give each student in group B a photocopy of page 62 (**Animal crossword: Student B**). Go through the meaning of *across* and *down*.

4 In their separate A and B groups, students quickly check the meaning of the words.

5 Put students into A and B pairs so that a student with **Animal crossword: Student A** is working with a student with **Animal crossword: Student B**. Tell them to sit back to back. They mustn't look at each other's crossword. They must exchange information to complete the crosswords.

6 Students take turns to ask for and give clues about the words, e.g. *–What's 17 across? –It's big and grey, it's got a long trunk. It lives in Africa and India. –It's an elephant!* Students write in the missing words.

7 Now tell the class they are going to read about a zoo. Do they know any zoos? What are they like? Pre-teach the following words and phrases: *demonstration, fall into decline, in doubt, in need of repair, resident, uncertain.* Give each student a photocopy of the **Questions** on page 63 and go through it as a class. Now give each student a photocopy of the article (**Uncertain future for town zoo**) on page 63. Students read the article quickly and answer the questions. Class feedback.

8 Divide the class into A and B groups. Tell them they have strong opinions about the future of the zoo: Group A want to shut the zoo; Group B want to keep it open. Give each student a photocopy of the relevant **Student A** or **Student B** role card from **Opinions** on page 63. Students read the cards in their groups and check words in dictionaries if necessary. They can add their own ideas.

9 Pre-teach some opinion expressions such as 'in my opinion'. Put students in A and B pairs. They discuss the future of the zoo and put forward their ideas. Monitor.

10 At the end of the activity, tell students there is good news. As a compromise, the council is going to build a new animal-friendly zoo outside the town. The students are going to plan it. Put them in groups of four to six. Give each group a photocopy of the **Zoo budget** on page 64 and a photocopy of page 65 (**Plan of the zoo**).

11 Tell students they have 500,000 euros to spend on looking after and feeding the animals every year. The cost of keeping the animals is shown in the **Zoo budget**. Students choose which animals they would like for their zoo but they can't spend more than 500,000 euros. They can have two groups of animals if they want, e.g. 2 x 2 tigers.

12 Students then look at the plan of the new zoo (**Plan of the zoo**) and decide where to put the animals. They can draw enclosures, write in the animal names or draw pictures.

13 Students tell the others in the class about their ideas using *going to*, e.g. *We're going to put the penguins in the lake.* Alternatively, put the plans of the zoo on the wall for everyone to look at.

Optional follow-up

Students write a factfile about a 'star' animal from their zoo. As a model, students complete the **Giraffe factfile** on page 64 and then write a similar text. Bring in animal reference books or research the animals on the internet.

Animal crossword: Student A

Ask your partner about the missing words on your crossword.
Give your partner clues about the words on your crossword.

			1 P				2						
			E			3 B	E	A	R				
4			N										
			G		5 O	6 W	L		7 P		8 C		
	9		U					10	A		R		
11 G	O	R	I	L	L	A			N		O		
			N						D		C		
					12				A		O		
											D		
13 T	I	G	E	R							I		
							14		15 M		L		
					16 D				O	■	E		
			17		E				N				
				■	E				K				
			18 G	I	R	A	F	F	E				
									Y				
		19											

Animal crossword: Student B

Ask your partner about the missing words on your crossword.
Give your partner clues about the words on your crossword.

			1				2 S						
						3	E						
4 L	I	O	N				A						
					5	6 W	L		7		8		
	9 D					H		10 P	A	R	R	O	T
11	O					A							
	L					L							
	P				12 Z	E	B	R	A				
	H												
13	I												
	N						14 C	A	15 M	E	L		
					16					■			
			17 E	L	E	P	H	A	N	T			
			A	■									
			18 G										
			L										
		19 L	E	O	P	A	R	D					

Uncertain Future *for town zoo*

The future of the historic zoo in the town centre is in doubt. After more than a century, this home to hundreds of animals might finally close its doors to the public. Opened in 1902, it was the first zoo in the country and welcomed thousands of visitors every week. People travelled long distances to see the exotic animals including tigers, lions and elephants.

However, in recent years the famous zoo has fallen into decline. Many of the buildings are very old and the number of animals in the zoo has dropped sharply. The larger animals such as tigers and camels are kept in small cages. Visitor numbers have also fallen with only two hundred people coming to the zoo each week.

The mayor said yesterday that he wants to close the zoo. 'It's very old and expensive to run,' he explained. 'It's not very popular with the public and it costs the town a lot of money every year. We're planning to shut the zoo and sell the land for a car park. The town needs more parking.'

Angry parents and town residents spoke out against the plans. 'We want to keep our zoo,' said one mother. 'There aren't enough places in this town to take young children. They learn a lot about animals there. The zoo just needs more money to pay for repairs.'

The council will decide on the future of the zoo at a meeting next Tuesday. A group of residents are planning a demonstration outside.

Questions

Are these sentences true (T) or false (F)?

1. The zoo is over a hundred years old. T / F
2. The zoo is going to close tomorrow. T / F
3. There are fewer animals in the zoo now. T / F
4. Thousands of people visit the zoo every week. T / F
5. The mayor wants to keep the zoo open. T / F
6. There is going to be a demonstration about the zoo. T / F

Opinions

Student A

You want to close the zoo because:

- it is old and small.
- the animals live in poor conditions.
- keeping animals in zoos is cruel.
- it is expensive to run.
- not many people go there now.
- people can see animals on TV and DVD or video.
- the town needs a new car park.

Student B

You want to keep the zoo open and spend more money on it because:

- it is an important part of the town.
- many families go there with young children.
- it is a good place for children to learn about animals.
- it is good for animal conservation; two baby tigers were born there last year.

Zoo budget

The zoo's yearly budget for feeding and looking after the animals is 500,000 euros. Which animals will you chose for the new zoo?

Wild animals	Cost per year (€)	Cost	Water animals	Cost per year (€)	Cost
2 tigers	100,000		2 dolphins	50,000	
2 lions	100,000		10 penguins	30,000	
2 leopards	100,000		4 seals	30,000	
2 elephants	100,000		**Farm animals**		
2 giraffes	80,000		4 cows	8,000	
2 gorillas	60,000		10 goats	4,000	
2 camels	50,000		20 chickens	2,000	
2 bears	50,000		20 ducks	2,000	
6 monkeys	30,000		**Children's section**		
10 deer	20,000		2 donkeys	8,000	
Birds			2 ponies	8,000	
4 eagles	40,000		10 rabbits	2,000	
4 owls	20,000		4 parrots	2,000	
					Total cost:

Giraffe factfile

Read the factfile. Complete the categories with the words in the box.

Character **Food** **Speed**
Did you know? **Height** **Weight**
Lifespan **~~Habitat~~**

Factfile

Giraffes are the tallest living animals in the world. There are only two species in the giraffe family. The other species is the *okapi*, which is much shorter than the giraffe.

1 ....*Habitat*.... Giraffes live in the savannas of East Africa and Southwest Africa.

2 .... A large male giraffe can weigh up to 1,900 kg.

3 .... The average giraffe is about 5.3 m tall but some male giraffes grow to 6 m.

4 .... Up to 25 years.

5 .... Giraffes are shy and peaceful animals.

6 .... Giraffes can run at 56 km per hour.

7 .... Leaves and small branches.

8 ....

- Giraffes are not only the tallest animals in the world but they are one of the heaviest land animals.
- The hoof of a giraffe is the size of a large dinner plate.
- Giraffes only sleep for a few minutes at a time.

Plan of the zoo

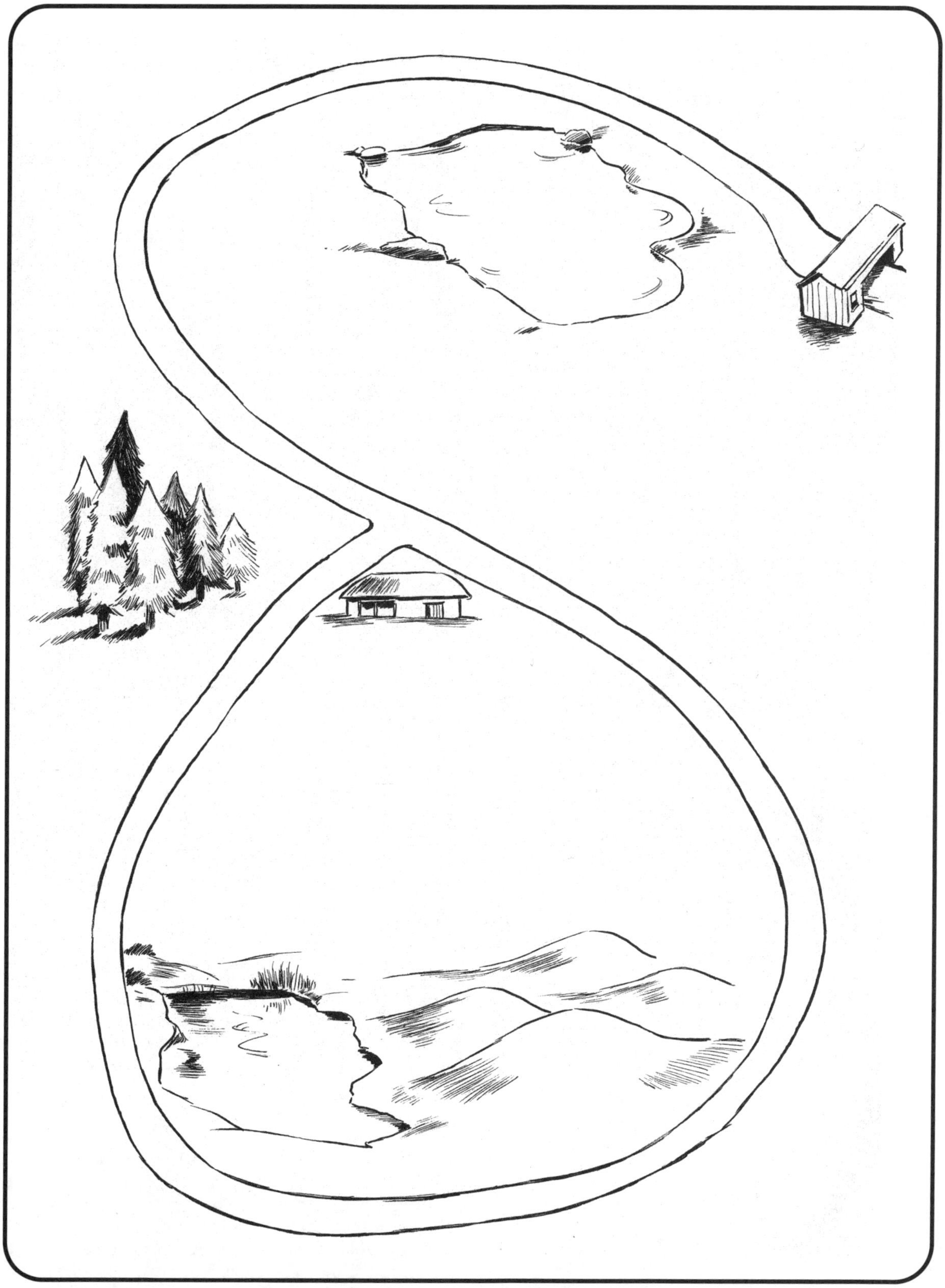

Project 14: Famous people from the past

Teacher's notes

Level Intermediate

Language Past simple questions, past simple, gerunds and infinitives

Time 180 minutes

Topic Biographies of famous people from the past

Skills development
• Reading • Writing • Listening • Speaking

Key vocabulary adore (v), assassinate (v), be born (v), break up (phr v), bring up (phr v), cut off (phr v), debate (n), devastate (v), fall out with someone (phr v), lifeboat (n), nationality (n), play (n), release (a single/CD) (v), reason (n), shark (n), ship (n), shoot (v), sink (v), tsar (n)

Materials
- Coloured pens, paper
- Monolingual or bilingual dictionaries
- History reference books (optional)

Before the lesson Photocopy:
- 1 page 67 (**People from the past** and **Now check your answers!**) per pair of students. Cut as shown.
- 1 page 68 (**The life of John Lennon: Student A**) for all students designated Student A.
- 1 page 69 (**The life of John Lennon: Student B**) for all students designated Student B.
- 1 page 70 (**The sinking ship debate!**) per student.
- 1 page 71 per group of students. Cut as shown.

The lesson

1 Ask the class about their favourite people from the past (the people must no longer be alive). Select some characters and brainstorm facts about them using the past simple, e.g. *He/She was born in … . He/She was famous for … . He/She discovered/painted/built … . He/She died in … .*

2 Give each pair of students a photocopy of the **People from the past** quiz on page 67. Go through the questions as a class to check any unknown words. Ask students not to call out the answers.

3 Students do the quiz in pairs. Give each pair of students a photocopy of the answers (**Now check your answers!**) on page 67. Brief feedback as a class. Which questions were the most difficult?

4 Tell the class they are going to read about John Lennon. Brainstorm what they know about him. Feed in information so that the class has an idea of the main events in his life prior to doing the pairwork activity. Pre-teach the following words: *adore, break up, bring up (brought up), devastate, fall out with someone, release (a single/CD), shoot (shot).*

5 Tell the class you will give them a biography of John Lennon with some information missing. They will need to ask their partner questions in the past simple to complete their biography.

6 Divide students into A and B groups. Give each student in group A a photocopy of page 68 (**The life of John Lennon: Student A**). Give each student in group B a photocopy of page 69 (**The life of John Lennon: Student B**). As a class, go through two example questions on the board. In their groups, students read the texts and identify what information is missing, e.g. dates, names of people etc. They prepare questions to ask for that information. Monitor.

7 Students now sit back to back in A/B pairs, ask questions and complete their worksheets. They can check together at the end and read through the text again. When everybody has finished, ask what they can remember about the events of Lennon's life. Listen for the correct use of the past simple.

8 Tell students they are going to play a game called **'The sinking ship debate'**. Give each student a photocopy of page 70 (**The sinking ship debate**). Ask what is happening in the picture. Go through the instructions at the top of the page. Tell students they are going to be a person from history; they must argue why they should go in the lifeboat.

9 Divide the class into groups of six to eight. Give each student a photocopy of a different famous person card on page 71. (Students could choose different famous people of their own.) Go through the expressions on page 70 and elicit what students could write, e.g. *I can read maps, I am good at sailing boats* etc. Remind students to use gerunds and infinitives appropriately. Now give plenty of preparation time for students to make notes on the worksheet as to why they should go in the lifeboat. Hand out bilingual or monolingual dictionaries if appropriate. Encourage students to use their imaginations. Explain who their famous person is if necessary!

10 Put students in their groups. Each student explains why they should go in the lifeboat. The others listen carefully. To finish they can have a debate and give further reasons why they are more useful/better than the others. At the end, each student has three separate votes for people to go in the lifeboat. Count the votes and see who the top four candidates are. The others have to swim!

11 In a subsequent lesson, students write a biography about a famous person from history. Refer the class to the John Lennon biography for useful verbs, expressions etc. Students may need to do research at home or use reference books. (Bring some to class.) Encourage students to write a 'best copy' of their text and decorate it. (Bring coloured pens to class.) When they have finished, read some out, but don't include the person's name. Students guess who the famous person is. Make a 'Famous people from history' corner in the classroom with the texts on the wall.

Optional activity

After students have written the biography of their famous person, other members of the class can prepare questions and interview them.

People from the past

Do the quiz and test your knowledge about famous people from the past.

1. Who was born with the name Norma Jean Baker?
a Eva Peron **b** Jackie Onassis **c** Marilyn Monroe **d** Greta Garbo

2. Which country was Cleopatra queen of?
a Greece **b** Egypt **c** Syria **d** Morocco

3. Who painted the Mona Lisa?
a Leonardo da Vinci **b** Rembrandt **c** Raphael **d** Velasquez

4. How many wives did the English king, Henry VIII have?
a two **b** four **c** six **d** eight

5. What nationality was Christopher Columbus?
a French **b** Italian **c** Spanish **d** Portuguese

6. Who wrote the plays 'Romeo and Juliet', 'Hamlet' and 'Othello'?
a Oscar Wilde **b** William Shakespeare **c** Charles Dickens **d** Rudyard Kipling

7. What field did Dr Maria Montessori work in?
a medicine **b** education **c** theatre **d** cinema

8. Who was the last tsar of Russia?
a Nicholas II **b** Alexander the Great **c** Ivan the Terrible **d** Peter the Great

9. Which painter cut off his own ear?
a Vincent van Gogh **b** Pablo Picasso **c** Leonardo da Vinci **d** Paul Cézanne

10. In which city in the United States was John F Kennedy assassinated?
a New York **b** Houston **c** Miami **d** Dallas

11. Where was Albert Einstein born?
a the United States **b** Austria **c** Switzerland **d** Germany

12. Who was Marie Antoinette married to?
a Napoleon Bonaparte **b** Charles de Gaulle **c** Louis XVI **d** Robespierre

---

Now check your answers!

1. Norma Jean Baker was the real name of Marilyn Monroe (1926–62).
2. Cleopatra VII (69–30 BC) was Queen of Egypt.
3. Leonardo da Vinci (1452–1519) painted the Mona Lisa.
4. King Henry VIII (1491–1547) had six wives.
5. Christopher Columbus (1451–1506) was an Italian, born in Genoa.
6. William Shakespeare (1564–1616) wrote 'Romeo and Juliet', 'Hamlet' and 'Othello'.
7. Dr Maria Montessori (1870–1952) worked in the field of education.
8. Nicholas II (1868–1918) was the last tsar of Russia.
9. Vincent van Gogh (1853–1890) cut off his own ear.
10. John F Kennedy (1917–1963) was assassinated in Dallas, Texas.
11. Albert Einstein (1879–1955) was born in Germany but lived in Switzerland and then the USA.
12. Marie Antoinette (1755–1793) was married to Louis XVI, who was executed in the French Revolution.

The life of John Lennon: Student A

Complete this biography of John Lennon.

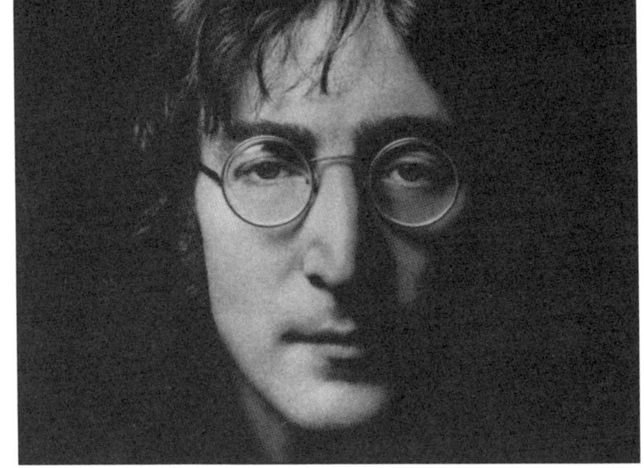

The Life of ***John Lennon***

John Winston Lennon was born in (**1**) .... (**where?**) on 9 October 1940. For much of his early years, John was brought up by his Aunt Mimi and his Uncle George but he saw a lot of his mother, Julia.

John's mother died when he was (**2**) .... **(how old?)**. She was killed by a car outside his aunt's house. Although John didn't live with his mother, he adored her and was devastated by her death.

John didn't do very well at school but he loved drawing and writing. After school he went to (**3**) .... **(where?)**.

John started his first band in 1955; it was called *The Quarrymen*. In 1957, John Lennon met Paul McCartney and together they formed (**4**) .... **(what?)**.

In 1962, the band released their first single called *Love Me Do* and then went on to have many number one hit records during the 1960s.

John married (**5**) .... **(who?)** in 1962 and their son Julian was born in 1963. After some years John left Cynthia for the Japanese artist Yoko Ono. They had a son called Sean.

In the late 1960s, John fell out with (**6**) .... **(who?)** and *The Beatles* broke up in 1970. John started a solo career and recorded the album *Imagine* in 1971. Many of his songs had a strong anti-war theme.

John left Britain and went to live in the United States. In (**7**) .... **(when?)** he was shot and killed near his apartment in New York by a fanatic. He was mourned by fans across the world.

The life of John Lennon: Student B

Complete this biography of John Lennon.

*The Life of **John Lennon***

John Winston Lennon was born in Liverpool on **(1)** .... **(when?)**. For much of his early years, John was brought up by his Aunt Mimi and his Uncle George but he saw a lot of his mother, Julia.

John's mother died when he was 17. She was killed by a car outside his aunt's house. Although John didn't live with his mother, he adored her and was devastated by her death.

John didn't do very well at school but he loved **(2)** .... **(what?)**. After school he went to Liverpool Art College.

John started his first band in 1955; it was called *The Quarrymen*. In 1957, John Lennon met **(3)** .... **(who?)** and together they formed *The Beatles*.

In 1962, the band released their first single called **(4)** .... **(what?)** and then went on to have many number one hit records during the 1960s.

John married Cynthia Powell in 1962 and their son Julian was born in **(5)** .... **(when?)**. After some years John left Cynthia for the Japanese artist Yoko Ono. They had a son called Sean.

In the late 1960s, John fell out with Paul McCartney and *The Beatles* broke up in 1970. John started a solo career and recorded the album **(6)** .... **(what?)** in 1971. Many of his songs had a strong anti-war theme.

John left Britain and went to live in the United States. In December 1980 he was shot and killed near his apartment in **(7)** .... **(where?)** by a fanatic. He was mourned by fans across the world.

The Sinking Ship Debate!

You are a famous person on a sinking ship with a group of other famous people. There is only one very small lifeboat with four places in it. You must decide who should go in the lifeboat. The sea is very cold and there are sharks!

Tell the other people on the ship who you are and why you should go in the lifeboat. You must give good reasons. For example, you can help entertain people in the boat or you know how to sail the boat and find land.

The name of my famous person is ....

Make notes using some of these expressions.

I should go in the lifeboat because ....

....

I can ....

....

I am good at ....

....

I can help people by ....

....

I know how to ....

....

If we have problems in the lifeboat, I can ...

....

You are **Cleopatra**
(69–30 BC)

Nationality: Egyptian

You are the very beautiful, intelligent and powerful queen of Egypt. You are good at organising people and getting thing done.

You are **Marilyn Monroe**
(1926–62)

Nationality: American

You are a wonderful comic actress. You are good at making people laugh and entertaining them.

You are **Marie Curie**
(1867–1934)

Nationality: Polish

You are a very intelligent scientist. You discovered radium with your French husband, Pierre. You are good at solving problems, making things and speaking different languages.

You are **Joan of Arc**
(1412–31)

Nationality: French

You are the famous woman soldier who led the French army in the war against the English. You are good at organising people, fighting and doing very dangerous things.

You are **Elvis Presley**
(1935–77)

Nationality: American

You are the famous 'King of Rock and Roll'. You are good at singing, dancing, acting and entertaining people.

You are **Leonardo da Vinci**
(1452–1519)

Nationality: Italian

You are a scientific and artistic genius. You are good at everything! You can paint beautiful pictures and design amazing buildings and machines.

You are **Christopher Columbus**
(1451–1506)

Nationality: Italian

You are a famous explorer. You are good at reading maps, speaking different languages and sailing boats.

You are **William Shakespeare**
(1564–1616)

Nationality: English

You are a famous writer. You are good at acting, reading and writing poetry and entertaining people.

Project 15: A class survey

Teacher's notes

Level Intermediate

Language Present simple, numbers and statistics, comparatives and superlatives, film vocabulary

Time 150 minutes

Topic Cinema and TV, lifestyles

Skills development
• Reading • Writing • Listening • Speaking

Key vocabulary animated film (n), actor (n), actress (n), cameraman/camerawoman (n), chart (n), costume (n), couch potato (n), director (n), (exercise) fanatic (n), government (n), half (n), horror movie (n), lack (of) (n), majority (n), make up artist (n), minority (n), overweight (adj), physical exercise (n), producer (n), quarter (n), recommend (v), romantic comedy (n), science fiction film (n), sound effects (n, pl), script (n), sound engineer (n), soundtrack (n), stuntman/stuntwoman (n), survey (n), three quarters (n), thriller (n), unfit (adj), western (n)

Materials
- Coloured pens, rulers, glue, scissors
- Monolingual/bilingual dictionaries

Before the lesson Photocopy:
- 1 page 73 (**Are we a nation of couch potatoes?**) per student or pair of students.
- 1 page 74 (**Hours spent watching TV every day** and **Weekly exercise**) per student or pair of students.
- 1 page 75 (**The wonderful world of the movies**) per student.
- 1 page 76 (**Write your own class survey**) per pair of students.
- 1 page 77 (**The results of our survey**) per pair of students.

The lesson

1 Ask the students the following questions: *How much TV does the average person watch every day? How much do they (the students) watch every day?* Generate discussion about the positive/negative effects of watching TV. Pre-teach the following words: *couch potato* (a person who watches too much TV and does no exercise), *exercise fanatic, government, lack of, lifestyle, overweight, recommend, survey, unfit.*

2 Give each student or pair of students a photocopy of page 73 (**Are we a nation of couch potatoes?**). Ask the gist question: *What is the problem with the lifestyle of British people?* Students read quickly and answer the question. (They watch too much TV, don't do enough exercise.)

3 Go through the true or false questions. Quickly revise the words: *half, majority, minority, quarter, three quarters.* Students read the article again and answer the questions. Pair check, then class check.

4 Ask the class how many people were in the survey (one million). Now give each student a photocopy of page 74. Tell them to look at the bar chart (**Hours spent watching TV every day**) and the pie chart (**Weekly exercise**). Check students understand *bar chart* and *pie chart.* Give examples of the following ways of expressing statistics: *X out of Y people* and *X per cent of people.* Now students look at the first bar of the bar chart. If there were one million people in the survey and 200,000 watch more than three hours of TV every day, we can say *two out of ten/twenty per cent of* people watch more than three hours of TV a day.

5 Students look at the charts and complete the sentences on page 74. Pair check, then class feedback.

6 Tell students they are going to do their own class survey about films. First, they will learn some 'film' vocabulary. Give each student a photocopy of page 75 (**The wonderful world of the movies**). Go through the categories and examples (*'elements of a film'* includes *soundtrack, costumes, sound effects, script* etc.). Do two further examples as a class. Put students in groups with bilingual or monolingual dictionaries. They complete the diagram. Feedback as class. Highlight that for some types of film we can use just one word: *a thriller, a western* etc. but we must say *a horror film*, or a *science fiction film*.

7 In pairs, students now prepare their class survey about films. Give each pair of students a photocopy of page 76 (**Write your own class survey**). Go through the worksheet step by step. Ask the class to do section 1 and write questions. Class feedback.

8 Students look at the two example questions in section 2. Highlight the fact that they have five possible answers: a, b, c, d, e. In pairs, students write two of their own questions (plus five possible answers) that they would like to ask the rest of the class. Weaker students could use one of the model questions and make up one of their own.

9 Students then carry out the survey in pairs. They mingle around the class, asking their two questions and noting the results with ticks in the table in section 3. Monitor and encourage the use of English.

10 Give each pair of students a photocopy of page 77 (**The results of our survey**). Students make two bar charts to represent the results of their two questions. (Refer students to page 74). Using rulers they can measure and add numbers to the left-hand vertical column to indicate the number of students. They can then draw and colour in five bars to show the number of students who gave 'a' answers, the number of students who gave 'b' answers etc. Students write the question at the top and write in the answers under each bar. Ask the class to cut out and stick their charts on a big sheet of paper for a classroom display.

11 As a follow up, students can make up statistics about their results, e.g. *Nine out of thirty people like science fiction films the best. Ten per cent of the class never go to the cinema.* They can also use comparatives and superlatives, e.g. *Brad Pitt is more popular than Tom Cruise. Brad Pitt is the most popular actor.*

Optional activity

Students make pie charts of their results using circles drawn on paper (see page 74).

Are we a Nation of Couch Potatoes?

For the first time, the government has had a serious look at the lifestyles of people in the twenty-first century. Are we a country of exercise fanatics or a nation of couch potatoes? William Burton reports on the biggest survey of its kind into how we spend our lives.

Last year government representatives questioned a million Britons on what they do in a typical day. It seems that eating, sleeping and watching TV take up half the day with only twenty minutes spent on household jobs such as cleaning or ironing.

One of the most surprising things to come out of the survey is the fact that over half the people questioned watch more than two hours of television a day. In addition to this, two out of ten people admitted watching more than three hours of TV a day.

Perhaps the most worrying aspect of the survey was the lack of exercise in most people's lives. Only a quarter of all Britons did some physical exercise twice a week or more, as recommended by the government. Most people said that they exercised once a week on average. However, an astonishing one in four people said that they rarely or never exercised.

Worried doctors are now predicting a sharp increase in the number of unfit and overweight adults. 'We must change our lifestyles right now,' said Dr Nathan Evans of the British Medical Organisation, 'or we will see serious health problems in the future.'

Questions

Are these sentences true (T) or false (F)?

1 The lifestyle survey is the largest of its kind. **T / F**
2 Over two million people were questioned in the survey. **T / F**
3 People spend three-quarters of their day eating, sleeping and watching TV. **T / F**
4 Jobs around the house take twenty minutes a day for most people. **T / F**
5 The government recommends people exercise once a week. **T / F**
6 Doctors think there will be more unfit and overweight adults in the future. **T / F**

Hours spent watching TV every day

Government survey of 1 million people

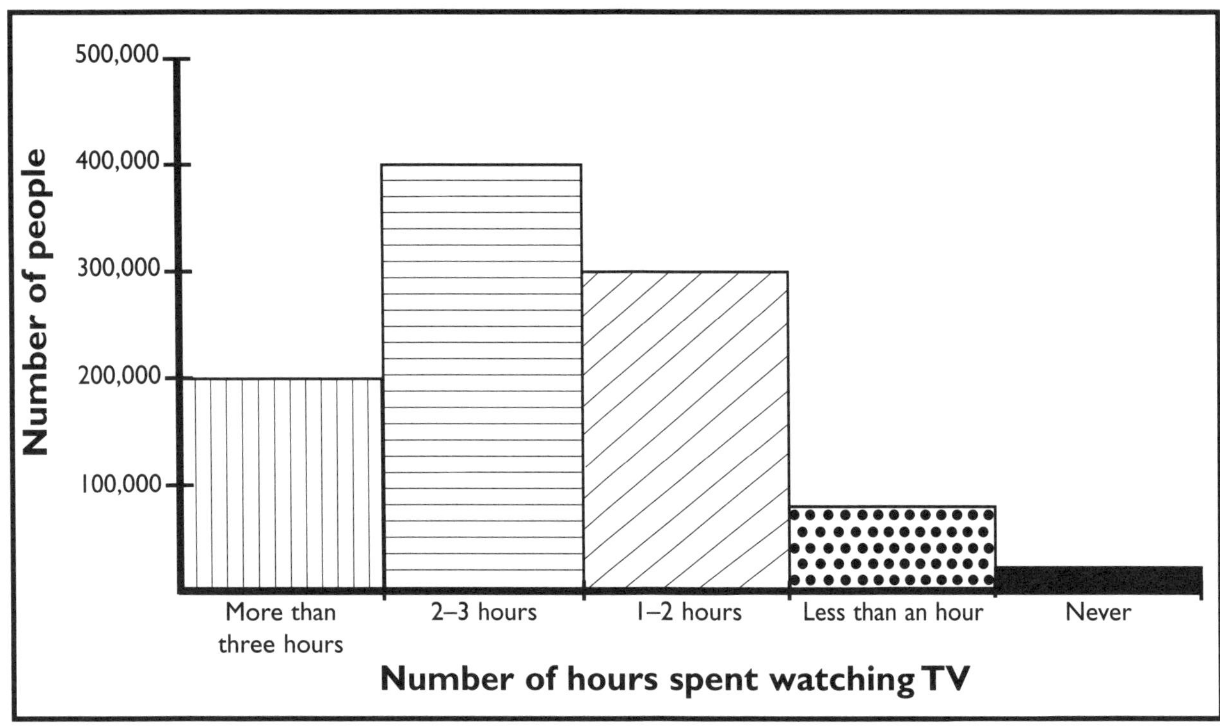

Weekly exercise

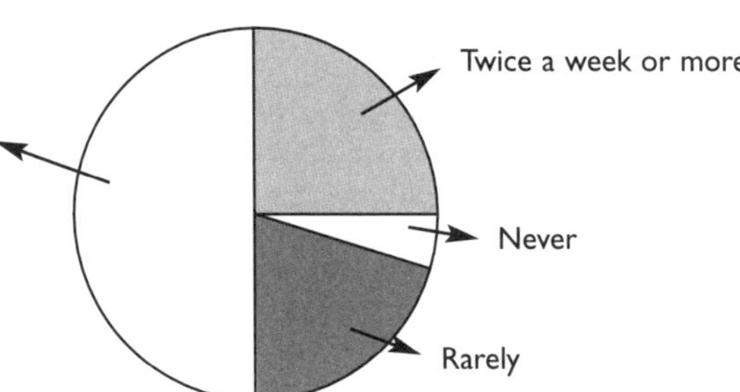

Look at the charts and complete the sentences with the words in the box. Use each word once only.

four
half
majority
minority
~~per cent~~
quarter
three
three-quarters

Watching TV

1 Twenty ...*per cent*... of people watch more than three hours of TV every day.

2 The .... of people watch TV every day.

3 A small .... of people never watch TV.

4 .... out of ten people watch between one and two hours of TV every day.

5 .... out of ten people watch between two and three hours of TV every day.

Doing exercise

6 .... of the people in the survey exercise only once a week.

7 .... of the people questioned did some exercise once a week or more.

8 A .... of the people said they rarely or never exercised.

The wonderful world of the movies

The words in the box are all connected with films. Write them in the correct place.

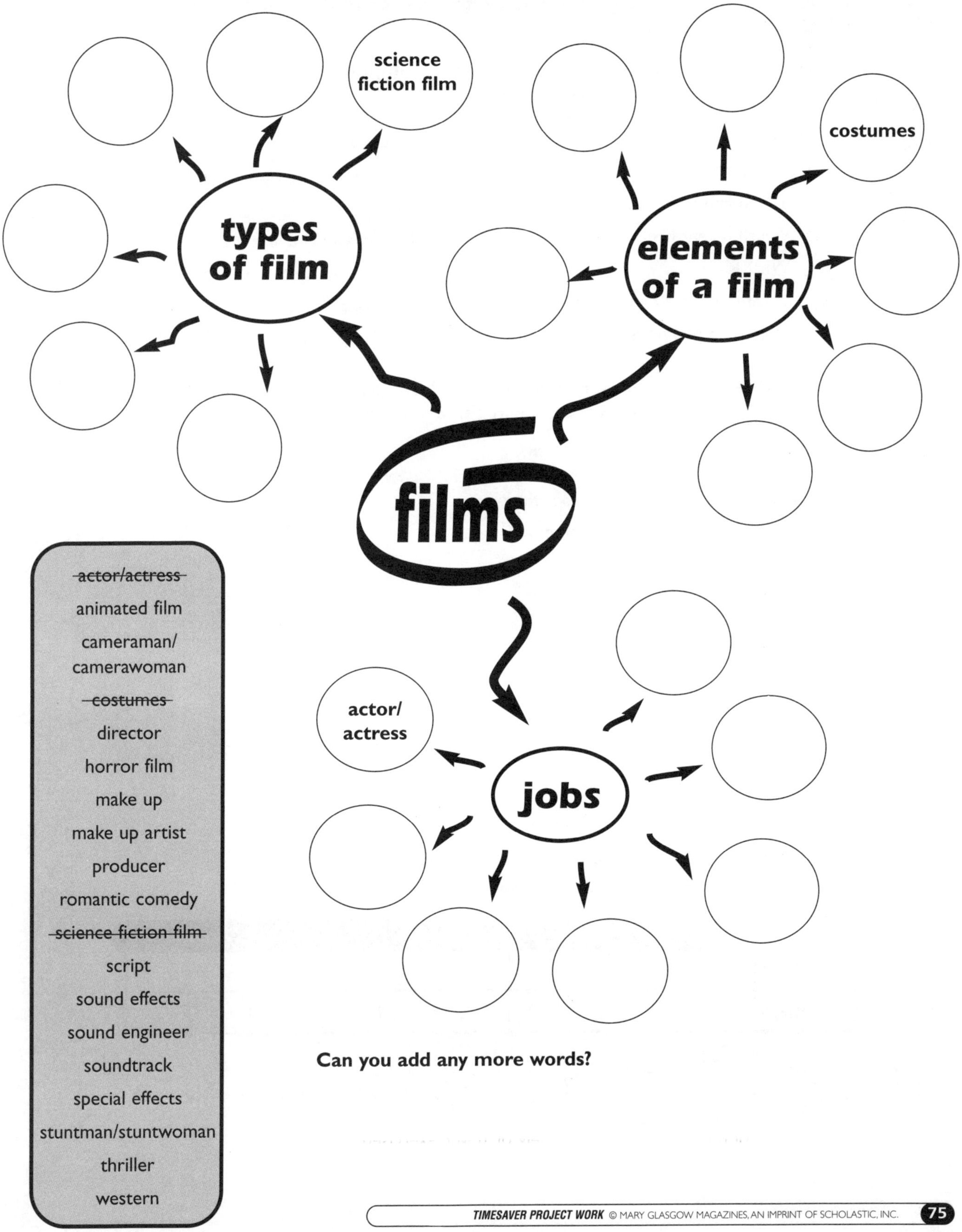

films

types of film
- science fiction film

elements of a film
- costumes

jobs
- actor/actress

~~actor/actress~~
animated film
cameraman/camerawoman
~~costumes~~
director
horror film
make up
make up artist
producer
romantic comedy
~~science fiction film~~
script
sound effects
sound engineer
soundtrack
special effects
stuntman/stuntwoman
thriller
western

Can you add any more words?

Write your own class survey

Find out what your class thinks about the coolest movies, the greatest actors or the best types of films. Discover how often they go to the cinema or watch a video!

1 First, write some questions. Here are some examples. Match A and B below to make questions.

1 ☑ d Who is	a like to meet?
2 ☐ How often do you	b your favourite type of film?
3 ☐ Which film star would you	c like to do?
4 ☐ Which recent film	d your favourite film star?
5 ☐ What is	e has the best special effects?
6 ☐ What job in the film industry would you	f to watch films?
7 ☐ Where do you prefer	g go to the cinema?

2 Now write two questions of your own to ask the people in your class. Include five possible answers. Look at the examples below.

What is your favourite type of film?
***a** horror film* ***b** science fiction film* ***c** romantic comedy*
***d** thriller* ***e** something else*

How often do you go to the cinema?
***a** more than once a week* ***b** once a week* ***c** once a fortnight*
***d** once a month* ***e** never*

Question 1 ....?

Answers ....

....

Question 2 ....?

Answers ....

....

3 Now ask everybody in the class your two questions. Put a tick in the right column for each a, b, c, d or e answer.

	Answer a	Answer b	Answer c	Answer d	Answer e
Question 1					
Question 2					

The results of our survey

Our Question ______________________________

Number of people

______ ______ ______ ______ ______

______ ______ ______ ______ ______

Our Question ______________________________

Number of people

______ ______ ______ ______ ______

______ ______ ______ ______ ______

Survey done by ______________________________

Project 16: Survive in the jungle

Teacher's notes

Level Intermediate

Language Past simple, present simple, jungle/survival vocabulary

Time 180 minutes

Topic Survival

Skills development
• Reading • Writing • Listening • Speaking

Key vocabulary battery (n), bite (bitten) (v), blanket (n), compass (n), crocodile (n), debris (n), fire (n), food (n), footprint (n), go forward (phr), go back (phr), hammer (n), hurt (v), in the distance (phr), jungle (n), match (n), path (n), raincoat (n), rope (n), rucksack (n), scissors (n, pl), signal (v), survivor (n), torch (n)

Materials
- 1 dice per group of students
- Counters (students could make their own)

Before the lesson Photocopy:
- 1 page 79 (**Crash in the jungle**) per student.
- 1 page 80 (**Game: Survive in the jungle**) per group of 3–6 students. Enlarge to A3 if possible.
- 1 page 81 (**Chance cards**) per group of students. Cut into cards as shown.
- 1 page 82 (**Chance cards** and **Survival cards**) per group of students. Cut into cards as shown.
- 1 page 83 (**My story – how I survived the plane crash**) per student.

The lesson

1 Ask students if they know stories about people who survived in the jungle or as castaways on an island.

2 Give each student a photocopy of page 79 (**Crash in the jungle**). Read out the introduction at the top of the page to ensure that everybody understands the scenario of the plane crash in the jungle.

3 Now tell students to match the words and pictures. Pair check, then class check. Pay attention to any pronunciation problems, e.g. *knife*.

4 Students choose eight out of the twelve objects to help them survive. In pairs, they can compare their lists and justify their ideas. Before this pairwork, quickly present: *I would take the knife because it's useful for killing animals/I would take the blanket because it's useful at night.* You could also turn this activity into a 'pyramid' discussion, with students making their own list, making a new one with a partner and then making one as a class.

5 Students now play the **Survive in the jungle** game. Pre-teach/revise the following words: *bite (bitten), crocodile, fire, food, footprints, go forward, go back, hurt, in the distance, path, signal (v).* As a class, quickly go through the game playing expressions on page 94.

6 Students play the game in groups of three to six players with a dice and some counters (they could make these themselves). Give each group a pack of 'chance' cards and a pack of 'survival' cards. They place these on the board in two piles. Tell students the rules of the game:
- Their plane has crashed in the jungle and they want to survive by reaching the 'survive' square in the middle of the board.
- The first person throws the dice and moves their counter the correct number of spaces. Students take it in turns to throw the dice and move their counters.
- Players need to collect one of each of the picture 'survival' cards: food, water and fire. They collect them by landing on the relevant square; they then take the relevant 'survival' card by looking through the pack. When they have collected one of each picture 'survival' cards, they can stop moving around the outside of the board and go up the middle path towards the final 'survive' square. Players keep going around the outer circle of the board as many times as necessary.
- If a player lands on a 'chance' square, they must take a 'chance' card, read it out to the group and follow the instructions (go forward/back, take/give back a picture 'survival' card). If they move to a food, water or fire square they can take the relevant picture 'survival' card.
- The winner is the person with all three picture 'survival' cards who reaches the final 'survive' square in the middle first. Players must throw an exact number to reach the final square.

7 Now give each student a photocopy of page 83 (**My story – how I survived the plane crash**). Tell students they are going to decide on their very own story of what happened in the plane crash. Go through the worksheet and check any unknown vocabulary. Tell students to complete their name and age (real or imaginary), tick one box per section and write in the most dangerous thing that happened.

8 Students now act as journalists who interview the person about their experiences in the jungle. Go through the questions needed to ask about the information: *Where did the plane crash? How long did you survive?* etc.

9 In pairs, students take it in turns to interview their partner and note down the information on a sheet of paper.

10 Students now use the information to write a short newspaper article about their partner's experiences. As a class go through possible headlines, e.g. *Teenager Survives in Amazon Jungle for Three Weeks* and elicit an appropriate paragraph structure. Encourage students to use direct quotes from their partner to make it lively, e.g. *'I thought I would never get out alive!'*

11 Students write rough drafts of their articles. Collect them and correct them. Ask the class to produce corrected copies, illustrate them with a picture and put them on the classroom wall.

Crash in the jungle

The plane in which you were flying has crashed in the middle of the jungle. You were the only survivor. It is daytime and the temperature is 35°C. There are trees everywhere but you can see a big river in the distance. There are strange bird and animal noises all around you. You decide to search the debris of the plane. You find the things below.

1 Match the words to the pictures.

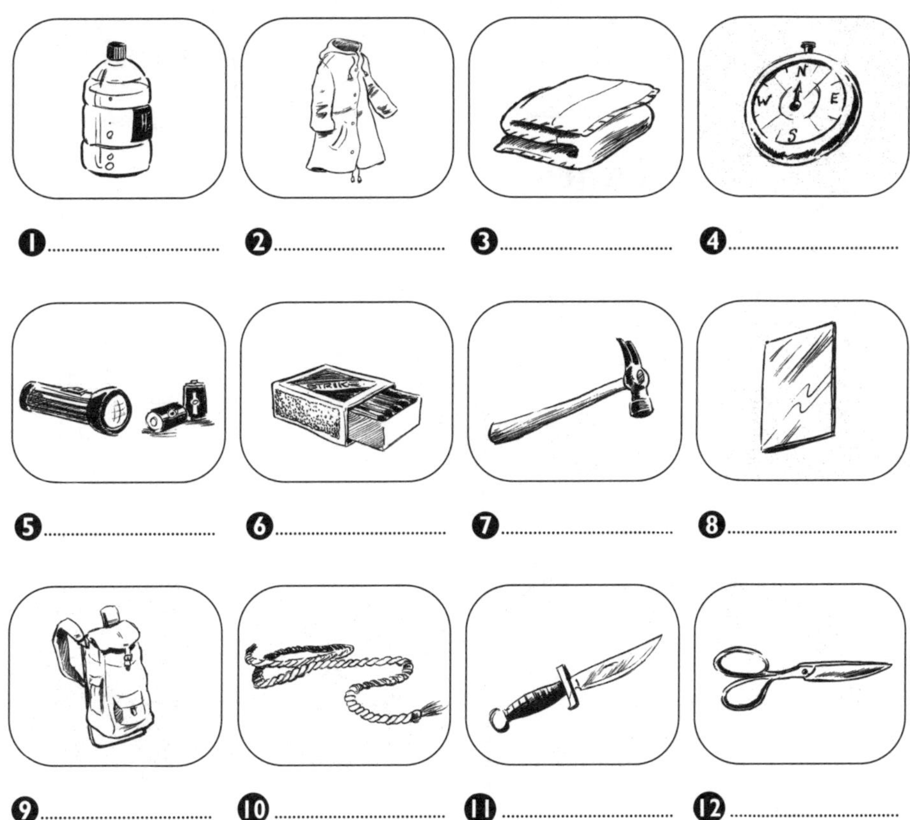

1 ....
2 ....
3 ....
4 ....
5 ....
6 ....
7 ....
8 ....
9 ....
10 ....
11 ....
12 ....

a blanket
a box of matches
a compass
a hammer
a knife
a large bottle of water
a large rucksack
a mirror
a pair of scissors
a raincoat
a torch and batteries
some rope

2 You can't carry everything. You must choose eight of the objects above to help you survive in the jungle. Write them here.

1 ....
2 ....
3 ....
4 ....
5 ....
6 ....
7 ....
8 ....

Game: Survive in the jungle

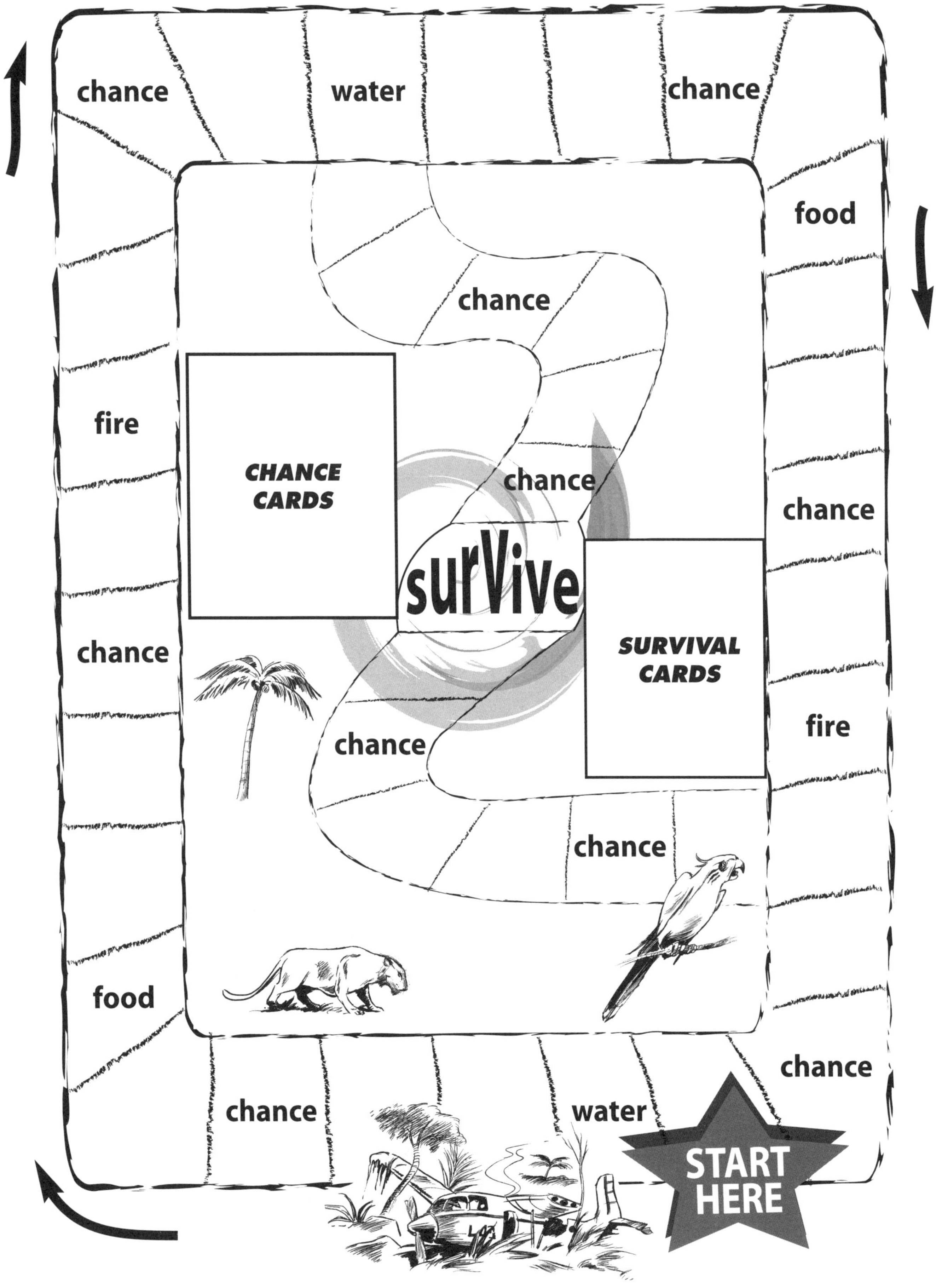

chance

water

chance

food

chance

chance

fire

CHANCE CARDS

chance

survive

SURVIVAL CARDS

chance

fire

chance

chance

food

chance

chance

water

START HERE

Chance cards

Take a survival card of your choice.

Take a survival card of your choice.

You must give back one of your survival cards.

You must give back one of your survival cards.

You must give back one of your survival cards.

You must give back one of your survival cards.

You are bitten by a snake. Go back two spaces.

You are bitten by a crocodile. Go back two spaces.

You knock over your water bottle. Go back two spaces.

You are frightened of the wild animals. You stay up a tree for ten hours. Go back one space.

You find some fruit to eat. Go forward one space.

You make a house out of leaves and sticks. Go forward one space.

You walk 50 km in one day. Go forward two spaces.

You build a small boat and go 20 km down the river. Go forward three spaces.

You eat some fruit and you now feel ill. Go back one space.

You lose your knife. Go back two spaces.

You are bitten by insects. Go back two spaces.

You hear strange noises in the night and you feel very frightened. Go back one space.

You climb to the top of a mountain and see a village in the distance. Go forward two spaces.

You find a path in the jungle. Go forward two spaces.

You find a pool of fresh water to drink from. Go forward one space.

You find some leaves to make a fire with. Go forward one space.

You climb up a tree and see some smoke in the distance. Go forward four spaces.

You find some footprints and you decide to follow them. Go forward four spaces.

Chance cards

You drop your box of matches in a river. Go back four spaces.

You lose your compass and you walk round in circles for two days. Go back four spaces.

You fall out of a tree and hurt your leg. Go back two spaces.

The batteries in your torch run out. Go back one space.

You see a plane and you signal with your mirror. Go forward seven spaces.

You hear some voices in the distance. Go forward two spaces.

You swim across a big river. Go forward two spaces.

When you are asleep somebody steals your rucksack. You are very frightened. Go back four spaces.

Survival cards

My story – how I survived the plane crash

My name is ....

I'm .... years old.

The plane crashed in the jungle in:

- ☐ the Amazon
- ☐ West Africa
- ☐ Indonesia
- ☐ India

I survived in the jungle for:

- ☐ five days
- ☐ one week
- ☐ three weeks
- ☐ two months

I ate:

- ☐ fruit that I picked from the trees
- ☐ nuts and berries that I found
- ☐ wild animals that I killed
- ☐ fish that I got from the river

I slept:

- ☐ in a cave
- ☐ under some bushes
- ☐ up a tree
- ☐ in a tent that I made myself

I escaped from the jungle by:

- ☐ making a small boat to go on the river
- ☐ swimming across a river full of crocodiles
- ☐ attracting the attention of a rescue plane
- ☐ walking 100 km and finding a village

The most dangerous thing that happened was when ....

....

....

....

....

....

....

My adventure story is now the subject of:

- ☐ a series of newspaper articles
- ☐ a best-selling book
- ☐ a major Hollywood film
- ☐ a new computer game

Project 17: A class website

Teacher's notes

Note: This project can be done without access to a computer or the internet.

Level Intermediate

Language A variety of vocabulary and tenses

Time 240 minutes

Topic Websites and magazines

Skills development
• Reading • Writing

Key vocabulary assignment (n), celebrity (n), catwalk (n), competition (n), congratulations (n, pl), daily (adj), discussion (n), earth summit (n), event (n), exercise (v), fanatic (n), fitness (n), fortnight (n), global warming (n), gossip (n), health (n), horoscope (n), island (n), journalist (n), milkshake (n), recipe (n), star sign (n), text (n), website (n), wedding (n)

Materials
- Paper, coloured pens
- Bilingual/monolingual dictionaries
- Computer with access to internet and facilities for designing web pages (optional)

Before the lesson Photocopy:
- 1 page 85 Cool friends per pair of students.
- 1 page 86 (**Questions**) per pair of students.
- 1 page 87. Cut as shown.
- 1 page 88. Cut as shown.
- 1 page 89. Cut as shown.

The lesson

1 Tell students they are going to look at the home page of a website for young people, called **Cool Friends**.

2 Pre-teach/revise the following words: *celebrity, competition, earth summit, fitness fanatic, fortnight, global warming, horoscope, the latest (news etc.), recipe, quiz, sci-fi (science fiction), star sign, TV series.*

3 Give each pair of students a photocopy of page 85 (**Cool friends**). Ask students how a home page works (you click on a topic/headline to go to a more specific page of the website, with more detailed information). Now give each pair of students a photocopy of page 86 (**Questions**) and quickly go through the questions. In pairs, students find the answers and write them on the worksheet. Board feedback.

4 Tell students that as a class they are going to make a website for young people. They will work in pairs or groups to write the individual pages. Encourage the class to think of an interesting name for the website.

5 Students look back at the home page on page 85 and choose two sections they want to write for – a first choice plus a second choice. Note the following categories on the board: *news, TV and films, sport, horoscopes, travel, celebrities, fashion, health and fitness, music, food and cooking.* Go through the categories, elicit from students which one they have chosen and write their names on the board next to the category. If you have too many people for one category, ask some students to go for their second choice instead. Encourage students to opt for less popular ones if necessary! If there are any categories nobody is interested in, they can be dropped from the website.

6 Pre-teach the following words: *assignment, congratulations, journalist, text.* Go through one example section from page 85, 86 or 87 on the board and explain to students they are journalists and need to choose a theme for their first assignment on the website.

7 Put the class into groups or pairs according to the category they have chosen, then give each group or pair the relevant photocopied section from pages 87, 88 or 89, e.g. **Fashion** or **Sport**. Students read the instructions and decide which topic they want to write about; note that there is a space for students' own ideas for texts. Monitor and help students with any unknown vocabulary. They can write their texts in pairs or on their own. Each pair or individual may produce one or more short texts.

8 Students now plan and prepare their materials for the website. You may need to set this for homework so students can research their texts at home/in the school library/on the internet.

9 Students write rough drafts of the texts in class. Note that you can find the following example texts in this book for students to use as a model:
- Quiz: pages 27 and 28, 35, 67
- Factfile: page 32
- Town guide: page 44
- Guide to a theme park: page 51

Encourage students to make their materials lively, fun and interesting. Bring in bilingual or monolingual dictionaries. Monitor and help.

10 When the rough drafts are finished, correct them. Give out paper and coloured pens, ask students to design their texts on paper to look like web pages. Put one student in charge of designing the home page and ask each group to submit a short information box about their website section. (See the **Cool Friends** home page.)

11 Put the finished materials on the wall and encourage students (and people from different classes) to read the different sections of the website.

12 If you have access to a computer with web page design facilities, get the students to put their materials on HTML pages. Set up your own home page and other pages. Put the website up on the internet. Students with internet access at home can show their parents their very own class website.

Home | Contact Us | Help | Newsletter

Cool Friends

Quizzes

Games

Prizes

Chat

1 News Flash!

The latest discussions from the World Earth Summit.
Can the planet survive global warming? Click here to find out what you can do to help.

2 Movie Madness

Find out about the new sci-fi series on TV …
Plus all the new films at the cinema.
Win free tickets for the scariest horror film of this year!

3 Sport Fever

Who has won the US Tennis Open?
Catch the latest from Flushing Meadow.
Plus learn all about David Beckham and other top footballers.

4 Happy Horoscopes

Look into the future with our daily horoscopes.
Click here for the special star sign of the month: Libra.

5 World Travel

All about … the Greek Islands.
Find the perfect island for your dream holiday.
Competition – win a fortnight trip to San Francisco.

6 Celebrity Lifestyle – The Very Latest Gossip!

Pictures from the Hollywood wedding of the year.
Celebrity quiz: test yourself and your friends!

7 Fashion World

What's on the catwalks this season?
Plus … the top ten jeans.
Prizes! Win a weekend trip to Paris Fashion Week.

8 Health and Fitness

How healthy are you?
Do our five-minute quiz and find out!
Fitness fanatics – meet the people who can't stop exercising!

9 Music

Find out all about the latest sounds from the dance floor.
Competition: your chance to win 10 cool rap CDs!

10 Fabulous Food

Click here for our fantastic chocolate cake recipe!
Plus make your own milkshakes and smoothies.

Questions

Read the website home page and answer the questions below as quickly as you can!

	Answers
1 In which section can you find out about making your own drinks?	....
2 What type of series is on television?	....
3 Where was the celebrity wedding?	....
4 Which footballer can you read about?	....
5 Which capital city can you win a weekend trip to?	....
6 What are they talking about at the World Earth Summit?	....
7 How long is the holiday prize to San Francisco?	....
8 What is this month's special star sign?	....
9 Which islands can you find out about?	....
10 What type of film can you win tickets to see?	....
11 What recipes can you find on the website?	....
12 How often do they change the horoscopes?	....
13 What type of CDs can you win?	....
14 What can you find the top ten of?	....
15 What problem do the fitness fanatics have?	....

The News

Congratulations! You have a job as a news journalist on a website for young people. For your first assignment you need to write an interesting news article. What type of news story is important at the moment? Think about events in your country or in another part of the world. You could write about:

- ☐ an important event in your country.
- ☐ a natural disaster such as an earthquake or hurricane.
- ☐ an international problem such as a war.
- ☐ a problem with the environment.
- ☐ another event, e.g. ....

....

....

The World of TV and Films

Well done! You have a new job! You are a television and film journalist on a website for young people. For your first assignment you need to write an interesting text about the world of TV and films. You could write:

- ☐ a film review of the latest movie.
- ☐ a quiz about the world of films.
- ☐ a short television guide with the best programmes on TV tonight.
- ☐ a factfile about a young film star.
- ☐ an article about a famous film star from the past.
- ☐ another type of text, e.g. ....

....

....

Sport

Congratulations! You have a new job as a sports journalist on a website for young people. For your first assignment you need to write an interesting text about the world of sport. You could write:

- ☐ an article about a football, tennis or basketball match.
- ☐ a factfile about a famous sportsman or woman.
- ☐ a quiz about the world of sport.
- ☐ a profile of a football club with information about the stadium, players and history of the club.
- ☐ an article about an unusual sport.
- ☐ another type of text, e.g. ....

....

....

Horoscopes

You are a person who can see into the future! You have a fantastic new job as an astrologist who writes horoscopes for a website. For your first assignment you need to write this month's horoscopes.

These are the star signs in English:

- **Aquarius** January 21–February 19
- **Pisces** February 20–March 20
- **Aries** March 21–April 20
- **Taurus** April 21–May 21
- **Gemini** May 22–June 21
- **Cancer** June 22–July 23
- **Leo** July 24–August 23
- **Virgo** August 24–September 23
- **Libra** September 24–October 23
- **Scorpio** October 24–November 22
- **Sagittarius** November 23–December 22
- **Capricorn** December 23–January 20

Here's an example of a daily horoscope:
Taurus You will have some unexpected surprises today. You might win a competition or get a phone call from an old friend. Just wait and see what happens!

Today's lucky number: 9
Today's lucky colour: blue

The World of Celebrities

Congratulations! You have a new job as a journalist on a website for young people. For your first assignment you need to write an interesting text about celebrities such as film stars, pop stars and famous sportsmen and women. You could write:

- ☐ an article about an important event in the life of a famous person (wedding, birthday party, birth of a child).
- ☐ an article about an award ceremony such as the Academy Awards (Oscars), describing who was there and what clothes they were wearing.
- ☐ an interview with a celebrity.
- ☐ a factfile about a famous person.
- ☐ another type of text, e.g. ....

....

....

Travel

Well done! You have a new job as a travel journalist on a website for young people. For your first assignment you need to write an interesting text about travel. You could write:

- ☐ a travel article about a country, city or region.
- ☐ a review of a new theme park or visitor attraction.
- ☐ a short tourist guide to a town, city or area.
- ☐ a list of top ten tips for travellers (for example, useful things to take on holiday).
- ☐ a shopping guide to your town or city.
- ☐ another type of text, e.g. ....

....

....

Fashion

Well done! You have a new job as a fashion journalist on a website for young people. For your first assignment you need to write an interesting text about the world of fashion. You could write:

- ☐ an article about the newest fashions for young people this season.
- ☐ a top ten list of the best clothes this year.
- ☐ an article about the latest designs for sports clothes such as football kits or trainers.
- ☐ an article about an event such as Paris or London fashion week.
- ☐ a profile of a top fashion designer.
- ☐ another type of text, e.g. ....

....

....

Health and Fitness

Congratulations! You have a new job as a journalist on a website for young people. For your first assignment you need to write an interesting text about health and fitness. You could write:

- ☐ an article about how to get fit – include suggestions for types of exercise (running, swimming etc.) and how long you should do them for.
- ☐ a quiz to find out how healthy people are.
- ☐ top ten tips for a healthy lifestyle.
- ☐ an article about the types of food you should avoid.
- ☐ another type of text, e.g. ....

....

....

Music

Well done! You have a new job as a music journalist on a website for young people. For your first assignment you need to write an interesting text about the world of music. You could write:

- ☐ a review of a pop concert.
- ☐ a factfile about a famous musician.
- ☐ a biography of a famous person from the world of music.
- ☐ a review of a famous musical.
- ☐ a quiz about the world of music.
- ☐ another type of text, e.g. ....

....

....

Food and Cooking

Congratulations! You have a new job as a journalist on a website for young people. For your first assignment you need to write an interesting text about food and cooking. You could write:

- ☐ an article about the special food and drink of your country or region.
- ☐ a simple recipe for biscuits, a cake or another dish.
- ☐ a quick guide to making a variety of drinks (milkshakes, hot chocolate).
- ☐ a guide to restaurants or cafés in your area.
- ☐ another type of text, e.g. ....

....

....

Answer Key

Project 1: Let's get started (pages 10–13)

Page 11, Classroom objects

1 a pencil
2 some felt-tip pens
3 a pen
4 a pencil sharpener
5 an elastic band
6 some glue
7 a dictionary
8 a paper clip
9 a pair of scissors
10 some paper
11 some sellotape
12 a rubber
13 a ruler
14 a stapler

Page 12

The four missing things are: a rubber, a pencil sharpener, a paper clip and some sellotape.

Project 2: All about us (pages 14–17)

Page 16, Questions

1 Fourteen.
2 Verona, (north of) Italy.
3 Basketball, football and swimming.
4 Blond.
5 Camille.
6 Antonio.
7 Italy, France or Spain.
8 Tidying her room.
9 Sylvie.
10 Antonio.

Page 16, Interview with Sylvie

1 What is your name? i
2 How old are you? a
3 What colour eyes have you got? b
4 Where do you live? g
5 Have you got any brothers and sisters? j
6 What do you like doing? d
7 What don't you like doing? f
8 What is your favourite food? c
9 What is your favourite colour? h
10 What is your lucky number? e

Project 3: Come to a party! (pages 18–21)

Page 20, Questions

1 Number 4
2 Number 2
3 Number 4
4 Number 1
5 Number 3
6 Number 3
7 Number 2
8 Number 4

Project 4: Design a new outfit (pages 22–25)

Page 24, Young designers of the year

(Suggested answers)

Alvin Shine designed the sweatshirt (number 1).
(He designed a similar big sweatshirt with 'New York' on the front.)

Marco Rossi designer the swimsuit (number 2).
(He designs sports clothes for men and women, including swimsuits.)

Ella McCarthy designed the dress (number 3).
(She designed a short dress for clubbing.)

Yvette Laurent designed the skirt (number 4).
(She designed a romantic skirt with large flowers.)

Marco Rossi designed the T-shirt (number 5).
(He designs T-shirts and also uses big black and white stripes.)

Ella McCarthy designed the necklace (number 6).
(She designs necklaces.)

Yvette Laurent designed the hat (number 7).
(She designs romantic clothes including hats.)

Alvin Shine designed the trainers (number 8).
(He designs cool trainers.)

Project 5: A class quiz (pages 26–29)

Page 28, Five-minute quiz!

1 h
2 c
3 f
4 n
5 m
6 b
7 g
8 q
9 d
10 i
11 k
12 j
13 a
14 o
15 l
16 p
17 r
18 e

Project 6: A famous person (pages 30–33)

Page 31, Brad Pitt

1	d	8	f
2	i	9	b
3	m	10	l
4	k	11	c
5	g	12	a
6	h	13	j
7	n	14	e

Page 32, Questions

1	T	4	F
2	F	5	T
3	T	6	F

Project 7: The Crazy Olympics (pages 34–37)

Page 36

1	e	5	a
2	f	6	h
3	d	7	c
4	g	8	b

Project 9: Where I live (pages 42–45)

Page 43, A map of Bridgetown

1	café	6	park
2	station	7	school
3	bridge	8	hospital
4	river	9	cinema
5	castle	10	supermarket

Page 45, Questions

1 40 minutes.
2 Dungeons (and the Singing Ghost).
3 1489.
4 Saturday.
5 Clothes, CDs, pictures and antiques.
6 At the Old Lion Hotel.
7 At the Olympia Hotel.
8 One kilometre.
9 The M23 9south of London) and the B216.
10 London Victoria Station.

Project 10: Aliens from outer space! (pages 46–49)

Page 47, Questions

1	c	4	b
2	b	5	a
3	a		

Page 48, Find the aliens
Students 1–8 aren't aliens.
Students 9 and 10 are aliens.

Project 11: A new theme park (pages 50–53)

Page 52, Three theme parks
Cadbury World
Theme: chocolate
Country: the UK
Number of visitors: Over 500,000 every year

Santa's Enchanted Forest
Theme: Christmas
City: (near) Miami
Open: From the beginning of November until January. 5 pm to midnight.
Number of visitors: Over 400,000 every year
Things to do and see: Meet Father Christmas, see one of the tallest Christmas trees in the world, go on the rides and see the magic shows, try different types of Christmas food and drink and listen to Christmas music.

Futuroscope
City: (near) Poitiers
Country: France
Open: All year round. 9 am to 6 pm
Things to do and see: See the latest advances in film, video, computers and the internet, including 3D cinemas and go on exciting rides.

Project 12: A new pop group (pages 54–59)

Page 55, Vocabulary

1	e	6	h
2	d	7	c
3	i	8	g
4	a	9	j
5	b	10	f

Project 13: A better zoo (pages 60–65)

Page 61, Animal crossword: Student A

Across:	Down:
4 lion	2 seal
10 parrot	6 whale
12 zebra	9 dolphin
14 camel	17 eagle
17 elephant	
19 leopard	

Page 62, Animal crossword: Student B

Across:	Down:
3 bear	1 penguin
5 owl	7 panda
11 gorilla	8 crocodile
13 tiger	15 monkey
18 giraffe	16 deer

Page 63, Questions

1 T	4 F
2 F	5 F
3 T	6 T

Page 64, Giraffe factfile

1 Habitat
2 Weight
3 Height
4 Lifespan
5 Character
6 Speed
7 Food
8 Did you know?

Project 14: Famous people from the past (pages 66–71)

Page 68, The life of John Lennon: Student A

1 Liverpool
2 17
3 Liverpool Art College
4 The Beatles
5 Cynthia Powell
6 Paul McCartney
7 December 1980

Page 69, The life of John Lennon: Student B

1 9 October 1940
2 drawing and writing
3 Paul McCartney
4 Love Me Do
5 1963
6 Imagine
7 New York

Project 15: A class survey (pages 72–77)

Page 73, Questions

1 T	4 T
2 F	5 F
3 F	6 T

Page 74, Watching TV and Doing exercise

1 per cent
2 majority
3 minority
4 Three
5 Four
6 Half
7 Three-quarters
8 quarter

Page 75, The wonderful world of the movies

Types of film
animated film
horror film
romantic comedy
science fiction film
thriller
western

Elements of a film
costumes
make up
script
sound effects
soundtrack
special effects

Jobs
actor/actress
cameraman/camerawoman
director
make up artist
producer
sound engineer
stuntman/stuntwoman

Page 76, Write your own class survey

1 d	5 b
2 g	6 c
3 a	7 f
4 e	

Project 16: Survive in the jungle (pages 78–83)

Page 79, Crash in the jungle

1 a large bottle of water
2 a raincoat
3 a blanket
4 a compass
5 a torch and batteries
6 a box of matches
7 a hammer
8 a mirror
9 a large rucksack
10 some rope
11 a knife
12 a pair of scissors

Project 17: A class website (pages 84–89)

Page 86, Questions

1 Fabulous food
2 Sci-fi/Science fiction)
3 Hollywood
4 David Beckham
5 Paris
6 Global warming
7 A fortnight/Two weeks
8 Libra
9 The Greek islands
10 A horror film
11 Chocolate cake (milkshakes and smoothies)
12 Every day/Daily
13 Rap CDs
14 The best jeans
15 They can't stop exercising.

Glossary of useful expressions

Playing a game

Starting off

Let's put the board here.
Who's going to start?
Why don't you start?
Where do we start on the board?
What colour am I?

Playing the game

A: What are the rules?
B: You have to …
A: Whose turn is it?
B: It's my/your/her/his turn.

Can I have the dice, please?
Take a card from here and read it out.
You have to go back/forward.
You can't do that! You have to …

The end of the game

I'm the winner!
You've won! Well done!

Working in a group or in pairs

Starting off

Shall we work together?
Have you got any paper?
Has anybody got a dictionary?
I'll make some notes.

Talking about ideas

That's a great idea.
I'm not sure if that's a good idea.

Making suggestions

Why don't we ask the teacher?
What about looking in this book?
We could put that picture at the top.
Let's colour in all the pictures.

Presenting projects to the rest of the class

Starting off

I'd/We'd like to present our project. It's about …
I'm/We're going to tell you all about …
We decided to write about … because …
We thought … was interesting because …

Showing posters

This is a poster/picture/map of …
We designed a poster/leaflet of …
As you can see, there is/are …
This picture shows …

Finishing

That's all! Thanks very much for listening.

Material written by: Janet Hardy-Gould

Project Manager: Howard Middle of HM ELT Services

Produced and edited by: Process ELT (www.process-elt.com)

Designed by: Studio Image and Photographic Art - Athens, Greece (www.studio-image.com)

Cover Photo: Pete Saloutos/Corbis

Illustrations by: Peter Standley

Printed in the UK.